# Bartending
## For the Professional and
## Home Entertainer

**BarBack Books**
**Maple Valley, Washington**

# Bartending
## For the Professional and Home Entertainer

## BarBack Books

BarBack Books are an imprint of:
The American Book Company
Post Office Box 948
Maple Valley, Washington 98038 USA

## www.BarBackBooks.com

The information in this book is true and complete to the best knowledge of the author. All recommendations, instructions, and suggestions are without guarantee on the part of the author or publisher. Always serve responsibly. Never serve minors.
The author and publisher disclaim all liability in connection with the information in this book.

This book is printed on acid free paper.

ISBN: 0-976-21981-6

Printed in the United States of America

# Bartending
## For the Professional and Home Entertainer

## <u>Table of Contents</u>

# Bartending
## For Fun and Profit

Most bartenders spend quite a bit of time hanging out in bars and nightclubs before becoming professionals. They like to call this "product research." My path was a little different, however. I became a bartender by accident.

My background is in the high tech arena. Until five years ago, my conversations evolved around programming code and the Seattle Mariners, I even carried a briefcase to work. Could life get any more exciting?

I decided to branch out a little, and began moonlighting as a teacher for a private college. This led to an assignment with a bartending school that wanted a new accounting system. I finished the job with no problems, but when it came time to pay me, things got a little interesting. To make a long story short, rather then pay my fee, they offered to put me through their school. Since the only drink I knew how to make was a rum and Coke (and I was little fuzzy on that), it sounded like an interesting proposition.

Learning the different techniques was a lot of fun. And when I found out about the potential money, I was really hooked. Forget the 9-5. I was ready to party!

My bartending career began less then 12 hours after I finished the classes. Some friends and I had stopped at a bar after work to relax and unwind. A few minutes after we arrived, the bartender got in a fight with her boyfriend and clocked him with a bottle of rum. Naturally, she was fired on the spot.

The nightclub was full of people, and no bartender! In seconds, there was total chaos. Screaming, gnashing of teeth, the whole nine yards. Seizing the moment, so to speak, I approached the bouncer and told him I could step in. I had not had a drink yet, and I had my license with me. The ink was still wet, but I was legal to work.

Ten minutes later, I was pouring drinks. My friends still laugh about it. I was totally lost. Learning in a classroom was very different from the pandemonium of a crowded nightclub on a Saturday night. It was noisy, crazy, I didn't know where anything was, and I loved every minute of it. Not only that, I made more in tips in those few hours then I made working three days behind a desk.

I became a regular bartender at that club, and eventually branched out to work in a variety of other environments. My experiences led me from black leather biker bars, to cozy family restaurants, slinky taverns, and glamorous casinos.

Customers were always asking me how they could get started in the bar business. It seemed everyone wanted to be a bartender, especially when they saw my tip jar. There were a couple of private bartending schools, but their fees ran upwards of $800-$1200. Most people who were looking for work didn't have that kind of money. There were also a lot of people who simply wanted to learn how to pour good drinks for entertaining friends and family.

With my bar experience and teaching background, I began developing a hands-on training program and textbook. To round out my skills, I also became a certified instructor with the state liquor board.

Fortified with my certificates, and a bottle of Jim Beam, I presented my program to several restaurants, colleges and technical schools. It was an immediate hit. Within a few months, the classes were offered in more then two dozen locations, and growing!

This book is based on the handouts and text I developed for the classes. With lots of good basic information presented in a straightforward manner, it is designed to be simple enough for the person who has never poured a drink, yet informative enough for the professional.

Bartending is a fun and satisfying career, and every day is different from the last. I hope you will enjoy it as much as I have. On this note, I have a suggestion for you. Keep a journal of your experiences. You are entering a unique world filled with comedians, drama queens, con artists, sitcom situations, and good old fashion nonsense, savor every minute of it.

# Bartending Basics

## Liquor Groups

1. **Vodka**

2. **Whiskey**
   a. American Whiskey
   b. Canadian Whiskey
   c. Irish Whiskey
   d. Bourbon
   e. Scotch Whiskey

3. **Gin**

4. **Rum**

5. **Tequila**

6. **Brandy and Cognac**

7. **Liqueurs & Schnapps**

8. **Wines**
   a. White Wines
   b. Blush Wines
   c. Red Wines
   d. Dessert Wines
   e. Sparkling Wines

9. **Beers**
   a. Domestic Beers
   b. Imported Beers
   c. Lagers
   d. Ales
   e. Stouts
   f. Porters
   g. Hefeweizen

## Mixers

1. Coke or Pepsi
2. Diet Coke or Diet Pepsi
3. 7-Up or Sprite
4. Cream (Half & Half)
5. Club soda
6. Ginger Ale
7. Tonic water
8. Bottled water
9. Sweet and Sour
10. Margarita mix
11. Orange juice
12. Cranberry juice
13. Pineapple juice
14. Grapefruit juice
15. Tomato juice
16. Coffee
17. Tea
18. Whipped cream

# Garnishes

1. Cherries
2. Spanish olives
3. Pickled onions
4. Tabasco Sauce - red
5. Lemon slices
6. Lime slices
7. Orange slices
8. Pineapple slices
9. Pineapple wedges
10. Peach slices
11. Celery sticks
12. Pickled asparagus
13. Grenadine
14. Rose's Lime Juice
15. Salt
16. Sugar

# Additional Supplies

1. Bloody Mary Mix
2. Tabasco Sauce - green
3. Piña Colada Mix
4. Fresh Strawberries
5. Fresh Peaches

# Types of Glasses

1. Shot
2. Rocks
3. Bucket
4. Collins/Tall
5. Hurricane
6. Specialty
7. Cocktail
8. Martini
9. Margarita
10. White Wine
11. Red Wine
12. Champagne Flute
13. Brandy Snifter
14. Pounder
15. Schooner
16. Half Schooner

## Sugared and Salted Rims

For best results, dip the rim of the glass in Rose's Lime Juice, than roll it in salt or sugar (depending on the drink) until the <u>outside</u> lip of the glass is coated. You can also use a lime wedge soaked in Rose's Lime Juice.

If you are using a commercial salt caddy, be sure the sponge is saturated with <u>fresh</u> Rose's Lime Juice. Keep a watch out for fruit flies that may be stuck to the sponge, and wash it regularly to prevent mold growth.

Do not use water to adhere the salt. It is not sticky enough, when the water dries the salt will fall off.

## Floating Liquor on Top of a Drink

Many drinks call for a float, lid or top. These are different terms for the same thing. To create this effect, make the drink according to the directions, leaving about 1/2" of room on top. Pour approximately 1/2 ounce of the requested liquor or topping slowly, in a circular manner. Try to pour slowly enough to avoid mixing the "top" with the drink.

Floating creates a very pretty effect when using contrasting colors, such as with a Tequila Sunrise or a Mai-Tai.

Here are some common terms for floats that can be added to a drink, in addition to the liquor already in it. For example, an *Electric* Long Island Iced Tea, or a *Screaming* Fuzzy Navel.

**Against the Wall** - Galliano
**Electric** - Tequila
**English** - Gin
**Gold Plates** - *Jose Cuervo* Gold Tequila
**Multiple** - *Frangelico*
**Screaming** - Vodka
**Texas Plates** - Tequila

## Measurements

# 1 shot = 1 oz

## Not all shot glasses are the same.

## Most people assume a "shot glass" holds a "shot," but that is not always true.

There are many sizes of shot glasses on the market today. You can't always tell the exact measurement unless you test them by free pouring or with a jigger. Even the name can be misleading. For example, what is commercially sold as a "2 oz shot glass" may actually hold 1-1/2 ounces when filled to the rim, and one ounce when filled to the line. A shot glass labeled "1-1/2 oz" may hold an ounce at the rim and only 7/8 ounces when filled to the line.

Don't trust "the line" to mark "one ounce." You will need to measure using another method, such as a jigger. Line or no line, the rule of thumb is to always test new glasses.

Many bars use the "7/8 oz to the line" type of shot glasses, so that when they fill the glass to the rim customers think they are getting "a little extra." Actually, they are just getting the ounce that they paid for. Using these "short shot" glasses, can really throw off your measurements for recipes.

---

If the drinks you make at home don't taste as good as those from the bar, one of the MAIN reasons may be that the "shot" glass you are using for measuring may not hold a single shot. It may be larger or smaller. Either way, your recipes will taste "off" since the proportions will be wrong.

---

# Free Pouring

Using a "4 Count Speed Pour Spout" (the most common plastic type), pour some liquor (or use water if you are practicing), into a glass. Count evenly to four as you pour (1..2..3..4..). Pour the liquor into a jigger, making sure you are using the 1 ounce side, Are you accurate? The liquor should bubble up in the jigger but not dribble out. Nor should the liquor be below the top of the jigger. If you have too much liquor, speed up your count slightly and try again. If you are short – then slow your count slightly and try again.

Once you can pour a good ounce quickly and consistently, change the glass sizes (rocks, cocktail, bucket, margarita, etc.). You may need to adjust your pouring speed. When you can pour a good ounce into any size glass, change the increments (1/2 oz, 3/4 oz, etc.). Next, try pouring with your other hand.

When you can pour different increments with either hand (and do it accurately, which also means hitting the glass at least most of the time), try pouring using both hands at the same time. Tricky, isn't it? Don't worry, just keep practicing. After a while, you will not even think about it.

Learning to pour a consistent "4 count ounce" will really help you when you are bartending. You will be able to measure your recipes into any size glass or blender without depending on shot glasses or jiggers. Good free pouring looks professional and allows you to work with increased accuracy, speed and efficiency.

Good free pouring techniques and accurate counting make it easy to create all kinds of cocktails, even with recipes you have never seen before.

# Some helpful increments to remember

| | | |
|---:|:---:|:---|
| 1/8 oz | = | *Quick* 1/2 count |
| 1/4 oz | = | 1 count |
| 1/2 oz | = | 2 count |
| 3/4 oz | = | 3 count |
| 1 oz | = | 4 count |
| 1-1/4 oz | = | 5 count |
| 1-1/2 oz | = | 6 count |
| 1-3/4 oz | = | 7 count |
| 2 oz | = | 8 count |

## Some Helpful Serving Terms

| | | |
|---:|:---:|:---|
| **Blended** | = | Mixed in a blender. |
| **Neat** | = | Served at room temperature. |
| **Rocks** | = | Served over ice. |
| **Shaken** | = | Shaken with ice and strained. May be served *Straight Up* or *On the Rocks*. |
| **Straight Up** | = | Served chilled (no ice). |

# Stair-Stepping Recipes

It is much easier to memorize recipes when you can stair-step them. Start by listing several cocktails that contain a similar base and note the addition of different juices and liquors. This is a fast and easy way to remember popular combinations.
Here are some examples:

| | |
|---|---|
| **Vodka-Cran**<br>1 oz  Vodka<br>2 oz  Cranberry juice | |
| **Sea Breeze**<br>1 oz  Vodka<br>2 oz  Cranberry juice<br>2 oz  Grapefruit juice | **Bay Breeze**<br>1 oz  Vodka<br>2 oz  Cranberry juice<br>2 oz  Pineapple juice |
| **Madras**<br>1 oz  Vodka<br>2 oz  Cranberry juice<br>2 oz  Orange juice | **Jamaican Breeze**<br>1 oz  Rum<br>2 oz  Cranberry juice<br>2 oz  Pineapple juice |
| **Sex on the Beach**<br>1 oz  Vodka<br>2 oz  Cranberry juice<br>2 oz  Orange juice<br>1/2 oz  Peach Schnapps | **Jamaican<br>Sex on the Beach**<br>1 oz  Rum<br>2 oz  Cranberry juice<br>2 oz  Pineapple juice<br>1/2 oz  Peach Schnapps |
| **Sex on the Beach<br>Hawaiian Style**<br>1 oz  Vodka<br>2 oz  Cranberry juice<br>2 oz  Orange juice<br>1/2 oz  Peach Schnapps<br>1/2 oz  *Midori* | **Jamaican Bikini**<br>1 oz  Rum<br>2 oz  Cranberry juice<br>2 oz  Pineapple juice<br>1/2 oz  Peach Schnapps<br>1/2 oz  *Chambord* |

| **Black Russian** | | **Black Jamaican** | |
|---|---|---|---|
| 1-1/2 oz | Vodka | 1-1/2 oz | *Myer's* Rum |
| 1/2 oz | *Kahlua* | 1/2 oz | *Kahlua* |

| **White Russian** | | **White Jamaican** | |
|---|---|---|---|
| 1-1/2 oz | Vodka | 1-1/2 oz | *Myer's* Rum |
| 1/2 oz | *Kahlua* | 1/2 oz | *Kahlua* |
| 1 oz | Cream | 1 oz | Cream |

| **Smith and Wesson** | | **Colt 45** | |
|---|---|---|---|
| 1-1/2 oz | Vodka | 1-1/2 oz | *Myer's* Rum |
| 1/2 oz | *Kahlua* | 1/2 oz | *Kahlua* |
| 1 oz | Cream | 1 oz | Cream |
| Splash | Coke | Splash | Coke |

| **Rootbeer Float** | | **Chocolate Cherry** | |
|---|---|---|---|
| 1-1/2 oz | Vodka | 1-1/2 oz | *Myer's* Rum |
| 1/2 oz | *Kahlua* | 1/2 oz | *Kahlua* |
| 1 oz | Cream | 1 oz | Cream |
| Splash | Coke | Splash | Dr. Pepper |
| Float | *Galliano* | Float | *RazzMatazz* |

| **Black Dane** | | **Dirty Mother** | |
|---|---|---|---|
| 1-1/2 oz | *Aquavit* | 1-1/2 oz | Brandy |
| 1/2 oz | *Kahlua* | 1/2 oz | *Kahlua* |

| **White Dane** | | **Separator** | |
|---|---|---|---|
| 1-1/2 oz | *Aquavit* | 1-1/2 oz | Brandy |
| 1/2 oz | *Kahlua* | 1/2 oz | *Kahlua* |
| 1 oz | Cream | 1 oz | Cream |

| **Brave Bull** | | **Milky Way** | |
|---|---|---|---|
| 1-1/2 oz | Tequila | 1-1/2 oz | *Buttershots* |
| 1/2 oz | *Kahlua* | 1/2 oz | *Kahlua* |

| **White Brave Bull** | | **Milky Way Cream** | |
|---|---|---|---|
| 1-1/2 oz | Tequila | 1-1/2 oz | *Buttershots* |
| 1/2 oz | *Kahlua* | 1/2 oz | *Kahlua* |
| 1 oz | Cream | 1 oz | Cream |

## Attitude

Bartenders come in all shapes, sizes, colors, and ages. Lots of people can make drinks, but to be a really good bartender it takes a special way of thinking.

### The top reasons a bartender gets hired?
# Friendliness
### and a
# Positive Attitude

### Want to increase your tips and enjoy your job more?
# SMILE!

---

### Act like a puppy, think like a cat.

Let people know you are happy to see them and want them to come back! Act like a puppy - full of bounce, energy, and playfulness. Puppies are great mood lifters because no matter what kind of day you have had, they are ALWAYS happy to see you.

Just dropped a tray full of drinks? Don't stress out. Let it roll right off you. Think like Fluffy. Have you ever seen a cat fall off a bookcase? They land on their feet, flick their tail at you, and walk away saying, *"I meant to do that."*

---

Trust me. Life is better
when you laugh more and stress less.

### *Make friends, make money, have fun!*

# Traditional Drinks

## Common Single Liquor + Mixer Drinks

Sometimes the name of the drink is simply a combination of the names of the liquor and mixer. For example, Whiskey and Coke, or Vodka and 7. For these drinks use a bucket glass, fill with ice, add 1 ounce of liquor and fill the glass with the mixer.

The cocktail's name may include a call liquor (for example, *Absolut*) or simply the type of liquor used (bourbon). When a call name is not mentioned, then a well liquor is assumed to be the requested liquor.

"Diet" in the drink's name usually refers to Diet Coke. For example, *Rum and Diet*.

### Common Coke Drinks

- **Captain Coke - *Captain Morgan* Rum**
- **Malibu Coke - *Malibu* Rum**
- **Velvet Coke - *Black Velvet* Whiskey**
- **Crown and Coke - *Crown Royal* Whiskey**
- **CC and Coke - *Canadian Club* Whiskey**
- **Christian 'n Coke - *Christian Brothers* Brandy**

### Common 7-Up Drinks

- **7 and 7 – *Seagram's 7* Whiskey**
- **Turkey and 7 - *Wild Turkey* Bourbon**
- **VO and 7 - *Seagram's VO* Whiskey**
- **CC and 7 - *Canadian Club* Whiskey**

## Common Soda Drinks (club soda)

- **JB Soda** - *J & B* Scotch
- **Johnny Soda** - *Johnny Walker* Scotch
- **Crown and Soda** - *Crown Royal* Whiskey
- **CC and Soda** - *Canadian Club* Whiskey
- **Velvet Soda** - *Black Velvet* Whiskey
- **Hennessy and Soda** - *Hennessy* Brandy
- **Absolut Lemon Soda** - *Absolut Citron* Vodka

## Common Tonic Drinks

- **Bombay & Tonic** - *Bombay Sapphire* Gin
- **Tanqueray & Tonic** - *Tanqueray* Gin

# Amaretto Drinks

## Amaretto Mimosa

Champagne glass, chilled. Shake with ice and strain:

1 oz   Amaretto
2 oz   Champagne (chilled)
2 oz   Orange juice (chilled)

Garnish with an orange slice.

## Amaretto Sour

Bucket glass, fill with ice.

1 oz   Amaretto

Fill the glass with Sweet and Sour. Garnish with a cherry.

## Bocci Ball

Tall glass, fill with ice.

1 oz   Amaretto
2 oz   Orange Juice

Fill the glass with club soda.

## Godchild

Rocks glass, fill with ice.

1-1/2 oz   Brandy
1/2 oz   Amaretto

## Godfather

Rocks glass, fill with ice.

1-1/2 oz   Scotch
1/2 oz   Amaretto

## Godmother

Rocks glass, fill with ice.

1-1/2 oz   Vodka
1/2 oz   Amaretto

## Godsister

Rocks glass, fill with ice.

1-1/2 oz   *Malibu* Rum
1/2 oz   Amaretto

## Pineapple Twist

Rocks glass, fill with ice.

1-1/2 oz   Amaretto
2 oz   Pineapple juice

# Bloody Mary Type Drinks

## Bloody Caesar

In a mixing glass, 1/3 filled with ice, combine:

1 oz   Vodka
2-3 dashes   Salt and pepper
2 dashes   Worcestershire Sauce
2 dashes   Red Tabasco
2 dashes   Green Tabasco (*** HOT)
2 oz   Clamato juice

Shake thoroughly, than strain into a bucket glass filled with ice. The rim may be salted if desired. Garnish with celery, limes, olives, and pickled asparagus.

Love a cold Bloody Mary, but hate the watered down taste when the ice melts? Try freezing cherry tomatoes, and using them in place of the ice cubes. For best results, stick picks into the tomatoes BEFORE freezing.

## Bloody Anna

In a mixing glass, 1/3 filled with ice, combine:

| | |
|---:|:---|
| 1 oz | Aquavit |
| 2-3 dashes | Salt and pepper |
| 2 dashes | Worcestershire sauce |
| 2 dashes | Red Tabasco |
| 2 dashes | Green Tabasco (*** HOT) |
| 2 oz | Tomato juice |

Shake thoroughly, than strain into a bucket glass filled with ice. The rim may be salted if desired. Garnish with celery, limes, olives, and pickled asparagus.

## Bloody Mary

In a mixing glass, 1/3 filled with ice, combine:

| | |
|---:|:---|
| 1 oz | Vodka |
| 2-3 dashes | Salt and pepper |
| 2 dashes | Worcestershire Sauce |
| 2 dashes | Red Tabasco |
| 2 dashes | Green Tabasco (*** HOT) |
| 2 oz | Tomato juice |

Shake thoroughly, than strain into a bucket glass filled with ice. The rim may be salted if desired. Garnish with celery, limes, olives, and pickled asparagus.

---

Serving beer over ice will reduce the carbonation. This helps reduce burping, and helps prevent customers from developing a "beer gut."

## Bloody Maria

In a mixing glass, 1/3 filled with ice, combine:

| | |
|---|---|
| 1 oz | Tequila |
| 2-3 dashes | Salt and pepper |
| 2 dashes | Worcestershire sauce |
| 2 dashes | Red Tabasco |
| 2 dashes | Green Tabasco (*** HOT) |
| 2 oz | Tomato juice |

Shake thoroughly, than strain into a bucket glass filled with ice. The rim may be salted if desired. Garnish with celery, limes, olives, and pickled asparagus.

# Brandy and Cognac Drinks

## Apricot Stone Sour

Bucket glass, fill with ice.

| | |
|---|---|
| 1 oz | Apricot Brandy |
| 1 oz | Orange juice |

Fill the glass with Sweet and Sour. Garnish with cherries.

The word "stone" means orange juice is added to make the drink less sour.

## Beautiful (a French Connection)

Snifter, warmed.

| | |
|---|---|
| 3/4 oz | Cognac |
| 3/4 oz | *Grand Marnier* |

## Hot Toddy

Large coffee cup, warmed.

    1 oz    Brandy
    1/2 oz    Honey

Fill the cup with hot water. Serve with lemon slices.


## Incredible Hulk

Large snifter.

    1 oz    *Hennessy* Cognac (bottom)
    1/3 cup    Ice (next)
    1 oz    *HPNOTIQ* (top)

Try to pour the *HYPNOTIQ* slowly, using the ice as a buffer, so it will not mix with the cognac. As you serve this cocktail to your customer, give it a quick stir with a long handled spoon. The entire drink will have a delightful color change from a pretty blue to a very strange shade of green.

---

If you don't have *HPNOTIQ*, try this recipe:

    1 oz    Vodka
    1/4 oz    Blue *Curacao*
    1 oz    *Hennessy* Cognac

---

## Stinger

Rocks glass, fill with ice.

    1-1/2 oz    Brandy
    1/2 oz    **White** Crème de Menthe

## Collins Drinks
### (Collins =Liquor+Sour+Soda+Cherry)

## Brandy Collins
Tall glass, fill with ice.

 1 oz Brandy
 2 oz Sweet and Sour

Fill the glass with club soda. Garnish with cherries.

## Country Collins
Tall glass, fill with ice.

 1 oz *Chambord*
 2 oz Sweet and Sour

Fill the glass with club soda. Garnish with cherries.

## Joan Collins
Tall glass, fill with ice.

 1 oz Brandy
 2 oz Sweet and Sour

Fill the glass with club soda. Garnish with cherries.

## John Collins
Tall glass, fill with ice.

 1 oz Bourbon or whiskey
 2 oz Sweet and Sour

Fill the glass with club soda. Garnish with cherries.

## Juan Collins

Tall glass, fill with ice.

    1 oz   Tequila
    2 oz   Sweet and Sour

Fill the glass with club soda. Garnish with cherries.

## Mother Pucker Collins

Tall glass, fill with ice.

    1/2 oz   *Sour Apple Puckers*
    1/2 oz   *Watermelon Puckers*
    1/2 oz   *Peach Puckers*
    1/2 oz   *Tropical Fruit Puckers*
      2 oz   Sweet and Sour

Fill the glass with club soda. Garnish with cherries.

## Pineapple Collins

Tall glass, fill with ice.

    1 oz   Pineapple Rum
    2 oz   Sweet and Sour

Fill the glass with club soda. Garnish with cherries.

## Raspberry Collins

Tall glass, fill with ice.

    1 oz   Raspberry Vodka
    2 oz   Sweet and Sour

Fill the glass with club soda. Garnish with cherries.

## Southern Collins

Tall glass, fill with ice.

    1 oz   ***Southern Comfort***
    2 oz   Sweet and Sour

Fill the glass with club soda. Garnish with cherries.

## Tom Collins

Tall glass, fill with ice.

    1 oz   Gin
    2 oz   Sweet and Sour

Fill the glass with club soda. Garnish with cherries.

## Vodka Collins

Tall glass, fill with ice.

    1 oz   Vodka
    2 oz   Sweet and Sour

Fill the glass with club soda. Garnish with cherries.

# Gin Drinks

## Gimlet

Rocks glass, fill with ice.

    1-1/2 oz   Gin
    1/2 oz   Rose's Lime Juice

Garnish with lime slices.

## Gin and Ginger

Bucket glass, fill with ice.

1 oz   Gin

Fill the glass with Ginger Ale. Garnish with a lemon wedge.

## Gin and Tonic

Bucket glass, fill with ice.

1 oz   Gin

Fill the glass with tonic water. Garnish with a lime wedge.

---

Tonic water was originally called *India Tonic Water*. It contains Quinine, and was developed to help prevent Malaria in the East Indian jungles.

---

## Gin Rickey

Bucket glass, fill with ice.

1 oz   Gin

Fill the glass with club soda. Garnish with lime slices.

# Kahlua Drinks

## Black Jamaican

Rocks glass, fill with ice.

1-1/2 oz   *Myers'* Rum
1/2 oz   *Kahlua*

## Black Russian

Rocks glass, fill with ice.

|         |        |
|---------|--------|
| 1-1/2 oz | Vodka  |
| 1/2 oz  | *Kahlua* |

## Brave Bull

Rocks glass, fill with ice.

|         |        |
|---------|--------|
| 1-1/2 oz | Tequila |
| 1/2 oz  | *Kahlua* |

## Cookies 'n Cream

Shaker glass, fill 1/3 with ice.

|        |                      |
|--------|----------------------|
| 1 oz   | *Stoli* Vanilla Vodka |
| 1/2 oz | *Kahlua*             |
| 1/2 oz | *Bailey's* Irish Cream |
| 1/2 oz | Butterscotch Schnapps |
| 1/4 oz | *Goldschlager*       |

Fill the shaker glass with whipped cream. Shake well. Pour the mixture, including the ice, into a large glass.

## Dirty Mother

Rocks glass, fill with ice.

|         |        |
|---------|--------|
| 1-1/2 oz | Brandy |
| 1/2 oz  | *Kahlua* |

## French Vanilla White Russian
Bucket glass, fill with ice.

    1-1/2 oz   ***Stoli*** Vanilla Vodka
    1/2 oz   ***Kahlua***
    2 oz   Cream

## Gold Bull
Rocks glass, fill with ice.

    1-1/2 oz   ***Jose Cuervo*** Gold Tequila
    1/2 oz   ***Kahlua***

## Golden Wesson (Golden Bulldog)
Tall glass, fill with ice.

    1-1/2 oz   Butterscotch Schnapps
    1/2 oz   ***Kahlua***
    1 oz   Cream

Fill the glass with Coke.

## Rootbeer Float
Tall glass, fill with ice.

    1-1/2 oz   Vodka
    1/2 oz   ***Kahlua***
    1-1/2 oz   Cream

Nearly fill the glass with Coke. Top with 1/2 oz ***Galliano.*** Garnish with whipped cream and cherries.

# Separator
Bucket glass, fill with ice.

| | |
|---|---|
| 1-1/2 oz | Brandy |
| 1/2 oz | *Kahlua* |
| 2 oz | Cream |

> Yes, you are correct. This is technically a Dirty Mother with cream, which would make it a "Dirty White Mother." The name was changed to a "Separator," because people ordering a DWM kept getting beat up.

# Smith and Kerns
Bucket glass, fill with ice.

| | |
|---|---|
| 1 oz | *Kahlua* |
| 2 oz | Cream |

Fill the glass with club soda. Garnish with cherries.

# Smith and Wesson (Colorado Bulldog)
Tall glass, fill with ice.

| | |
|---|---|
| 1-1/2 oz | Vodka |
| 1/2 oz | *Kahlua* |
| 1 oz | Cream |

Fill the glass with Coke.

# White Jamaican
Bucket glass, fill with ice.

| | |
|---|---|
| 1-1/2 oz | *Myers'* Rum |
| 1/2 oz | *Kahlua* |
| 2 oz | Cream |

## White Russian
Bucket glass, fill with ice.

| | |
|---|---|
| 1-1/2 oz | Vodka |
| 1/2 oz | *Kahlua* |
| 2 oz | Cream |

## White Bull
Bucket glass, fill with ice.

| | |
|---|---|
| 1-1/2 oz | Tequila |
| 1/2 oz | *Kahlua* |
| 2 oz | Cream |

## Liqueur Drinks

## Adios Mother Pucker
Tall glass, fill with ice.

| | |
|---|---|
| 1/4 oz | *Watermelon Puckers* |
| 1/4 oz | *Peach Puckers* |
| 1/4 oz | *Sour Apple Puckers* |
| 1 oz | Vodka |

Fill the glass with even mix of 7-Up and club soda. Garnish with cherries.

## Alabama Slammer
Tall glass, or small pitcher, fill with ice.

| | |
|---|---|
| 1 oz | Sloe Gin |
| 1/2 oz | *Southern Comfort* |

Fill the rest of the glass with orange juice and top with 1/2 oz Crème de Banana. Garnish with cherries and orange slices.

## Fuzzy Navel

Tall glass, fill with ice.

1 oz   Peach Schnapps

Fill the glass with orange juice. Garnish with cherries.

## Honey Dew

Tall glass, fill with ice.

1-1/2 oz   *Midori*

Nearly fill the glass with lemonade. Top with 1/2 oz chilled champagne. Garnish with cherries.

> A drink made with *orange juice* often takes the name of the liqueur or liquor, followed by *"Driver"* or *"Navel."*

## Jolly Rancher - Sour Apple

Tall glass, fill with ice.

1 oz   *Sour Apple Puckers*

Fill the glass with even mix of 7-Up and club soda. Garnish with cherries.

## Jolly Rancher - Watermelon

Tall glass, fill with ice.

1 oz   *Watermelon Puckers*

Fill the glass with even mix of 7-Up and club soda. Garnish with cherries.

## *Midori* Driver

Tall glass, fill with ice.

1 oz   *Midori*

Fill the glass with orange juice.

## Midori Sour

Bucket glass, fill with ice.

1 oz   *Midori*

Fill the glass with Sweet and Sour. Garnish with a cherry.

## Mother Pucker

Tall glass, fill with ice.

1/2 oz   *Watermelon Puckers*
1/2 oz   *Peach Puckers*
1/2 oz   *Sour Apple Puckers*
1/2 oz   *Tropical Fruit Puckers*

Fill the glass with even mix of 7-Up and club soda. Garnish with cherries.

## Screaming Fuzzy Navel

Tall glass, fill with ice.

1 oz   Peach Schnapps

Nearly fill the glass with orange juice. Top with 1/2 oz of vodka. Garnish with cherries.

The term "**screaming**" means 1/2 ounce of vodka is floated on top of the drink.

# Sloe Gin Fizz

Tall glass, fill with ice.

> 1 oz   Sloe Gin
> 2 oz   Sweet and Sour

Fill the glass with club soda. Garnish with cherries.

# Slow Screw

Tall glass, fill with ice.

> 1 oz   Sloe Gin

Fill the glass with orange juice. Garnish with cherries.

> Sloe Gin is not actually a gin. It is a liqueur made from Sloeberries, a European berry similar to a wild raspberry.

# Slow Screw *Against the Wall*

Tall glass, fill with ice.

> 1 oz   Sloe Gin

Nearly fill the glass with orange juice. Top with 1/2 oz *Galliano*. Garnish with cherries.

> The term "against the wall" means 1/2 oz of *Galliano* is floated on top of the drink.

# Slow Comfortable Screw

Tall glass, fill with ice.

> 1 oz   Sloe Gin
> 1/2 oz   *Southern Comfort*

Fill the glass with orange juice. Garnish with cherries.

## SoCo Driver

Tall glass, fill with ice.

1 oz   *Southern Comfort*

Fill the glass with orange juice.

# Rum Drinks

## Banana Daiquiri

In a blender combine:

| | |
|---|---|
| 1/3 cup | Ice |
| 1 oz | *Malibu* Coconut Rum |
| 1/4 oz | Grenadine |
| 1/2 cup | Bananas |
| 1/2 oz | Banana flavored syrup |
| 1/4 oz | Coconut flavored syrup |
| 2 oz | Sweet and Sour |

Blend until the drink is a smooth slush. Serve in a chilled cocktail or specialty glass. Garnish with banana slices.

## Between the Sheets

Cocktail glass, chilled, no ice. Shake with ice and strain:

| | |
|---|---|
| 1/2 oz | Triple Sec |
| 1/2 oz | Rum |
| 1/2 oz | Brandy |
| 2 oz | Sweet and Sour |

## Blackberry Daiquiri

In a blender combine:

| | |
|---|---|
| 1/3 cup | Ice |
| 1 oz | *Bacardi* Light Rum |
| 1/4 oz | Grenadine |
| 1-1/2 cup | Fresh blackberries |
| 1/2 oz | Blackberry flavored syrup |
| 2 oz | Sweet and Sour |

Blend until the drink is a smooth slush. Serve in a chilled cocktail or specialty glass. Garnish with blackberries.

## Cuba Libre

Bucket glass, fill with ice.

1 oz   Rum

Fill the glass with Coke. Squeeze a lime wedge into the drink, and garnish with lime slices.

## Daiquiri

In a blender combine:

| | |
|---|---|
| 1/3 cup | Ice |
| 1 oz | *Bacardi* Light Rum |
| 1/4 oz | Grenadine |
| 2 oz | Sweet and Sour |

Blend until the drink is a smooth slush. Serve in a chilled cocktail or specialty glass. Garnish with cherries.

---

A few drops of Bitters on a lime wedge will stop hiccups almost every time.

---

## *HPNOTIQ* Blitz

Bucket glass, fill with ice.

| | |
|---|---|
| 1 oz | *HPNOTIQ* |
| 1/2 oz | *Malibu* Coconut Rum |
| Splash | Pineapple juice |
| Splash | Blue *Curacao* |

Garnish with a pineapple slice.

## Mango Daiquiri

In a blender combine:

| | |
|---|---|
| 1/3 cup | Ice |
| 1 oz | Mango Rum |
| 1/4 oz | Grenadine |
| 1/2 cup | Mango chunks |
| 1/2 oz | Mango flavored syrup |
| 1/4 oz | Peach flavored syrup |
| 2 oz | Sweet and Sour |

Blend until the drink is a smooth slush. Serve in a chilled cocktail or specialty glass. Garnish with mango slices.

## Mango Driver

Tall glass, fill with ice.

1 oz   Mango Rum

Fill the glass with orange juice.

---

**Bad Pick-Up Line**
If you were any more beautiful, you would be ugly.

# Peach Daiquiri

In a blender combine:

| | |
|---|---|
| 1/3 cup | Ice |
| 1 oz | *Bacardi* Light Rum |
| 1/4 oz | Grenadine |
| 1-1/2 cup | Fresh peaches |
| 1/2 oz | Peach flavored syrup |
| 2 oz | Sweet and Sour |

Blend until the drink is a smooth slush. Serve in a chilled cocktail or specialty glass. Garnish with peach slices.

# Pineapple Boo (Pine Boo)

Tall glass, fill with ice.

| | |
|---|---|
| 1 oz | *Malibu* Coconut Rum |

Fill the glass with pineapple juice.

# Pineapple Daiquiri

In a blender combine:

| | |
|---|---|
| 1/3 cup | Ice |
| 1 oz | *Malibu* Pineapple Rum |
| 1/4 oz | Grenadine |
| 1/2 cup | Pineapple chunks |
| 1/2 oz | Banana flavored syrup |
| 1/4 oz | Coconut or pineapple flavored syrup |
| 2 oz | Sweet and Sour |

Blend until the drink is a smooth slush. Serve in a chilled cocktail or specialty glass. Garnish with grenadine and pineapple wedges.

# Rum and Coke

Bucket glass, fill with ice.

1 oz   Rum

Fill the glass with Coke.

> Any hard liquor can be mixed with Coke, such as whiskey and Coke, or vodka and Coke.

# Strawberry Daiquiri

In a blender combine:

| | |
|---|---|
| 1/3 cup | Ice |
| 1 oz | *Malibu* Coconut Rum |
| 1/4 oz | Grenadine |
| 1-1/2 cup | Fresh or frozen strawberries |
| 1/2 oz | Strawberry flavored syrup |
| 2 oz | Sweet and Sour |

Blend until the drink is a smooth slush. Serve in a chilled cocktail or specialty glass. Garnish with strawberries.

## Tequila Drinks

# Cactus Cooler

Tall glass, fill with ice.

1 oz   Tequila

Nearly fill the glass with orange juice. Top with 1/2 oz *Galliano*.

## Tequila Driver

Tall glass, fill with ice.

1 oz    Tequila

Fill the glass with orange juice.

## Tequila Sunrise

Tall glass, fill with ice.

1 oz    Tequila

Nearly fill the glass with orange juice. Top with 1/2 oz grenadine. Garnish with cherries and orange slices.

## Tequila Sunset

Tall glass, fill with ice.

1/2 oz    Blackberry Brandy (on the bottom)
  1 oz    Tequila

Fill the glass with orange juice. Garnish with cherries and orange slices.

# Vodka Drinks

## Brass Monkey

Bucket glass, fill with ice.

1/2 oz    Vodka
1/2 oz    Rum

Fill the glass with orange juice. Garnish with cherries and orange slices.

## Bay Breeze

Tall glass, fill with ice.

   1 oz   Vodka

Fill the glass with equal parts pineapple and cranberry juice. Garnish with cherries and orange slices.

## Chocolate Monkey

Shaker glass, fill 1/3 with ice.

   1 oz   *Stoli* Vanilla Vodka
   1/2 oz   Crème de Cacao
   1/2 oz   *99 Bananas*

Fill the shaker glass the rest of the way with whipped cream. Shake well. Pour the mixture, including the ice, into a large glass.

## Grape Knee High (NEHI) 1

Tall glass, fill with ice.

   1 oz   Raspberry Vodka
   1 oz   *Chambord*
   2 oz   Sweet and Sour

Fill the glass with club soda.

## Grape Knee High (NEHI) 2

Tall glass, fill with ice.

   1/2 oz   Vodka
   1 oz   *Chambord*
   1/2 oz   Gin
   2 oz   Sweet and Sour

Fill the glass with club soda.

# Greyhound

Tall glass, fill with ice.

    1 oz    Vodka

Fill the glass with grapefruit juice.

# Harvey Wallbanger

Tall glass, fill with ice.

    1 oz    Vodka

Nearly fill the glass with orange juice. Top with 1/2 oz *Galliano*.

# Hawaiian Driver

Tall glass, fill with ice.

    1 oz    Vodka

Fill the glass with equal parts orange juice and pineapple juice.

# Hot Vodka Toddy

Large coffee cup, warmed.

    1 oz    Orange or Lemon Vodka
    1/2 oz    Honey

Fill the cup with hot water. A tea bag may be added. Serve with lemon slices.

# Madras

Tall glass, fill with ice.

    1 oz    Vodka

Fill the glass with even mix of orange and cranberry juice. Garnish with cherries.

## Melon Ball

Tall glass, fill with ice.

    1 oz    Vodka

Nearly fill the glass with orange juice. Top with 1/2 oz *Midori.*

## Salty Dog

Tall glass, salted rim, fill with ice.

    1 oz    Vodka

Fill the glass with grapefruit juice.

## Screw Driver

Tall glass, fill with ice.

    1 oz    Vodka

Fill the glass with orange juice.

## Sea Breeze

Tall glass, fill with ice.

    1 oz    Vodka

Fill the glass with an even mix of grapefruit and cranberry juice. Garnish with cherries.

## Sex on the Beach

Tall glass, fill with ice.

    1 oz    Vodka
    1/2 oz   Peach Schnapps

Fill the glass with even mix of orange and cranberry juice. Garnish with cherries.

# Sex on the Beach – Hawaiian Style
Tall glass, fill with ice.

    1 oz   Vodka
  1/2 oz  Peach Schnapps
  1/4 oz  *Midori*

Fill the glass with even mix of orange and cranberry juice. Garnish with cherries.

# Sex on the Beach with a Georgia Peach
Tall glass, fill with ice.

    1 oz  *Stoli* Vanilla Vodka
  1/2 oz  Peach Schnapps
  1/4 oz  *Chambord*

Fill the glass with even mix of orange and cranberry juice. Garnish with cherries.

# Vodka-Cranberry (Cape Cod)
Tall glass, fill with ice.

    1 oz   Vodka

Fill the glass with cranberry juice. Garnish with lime slices.

# Vodka Creamsickle
Tall glass, fill with ice.

    1 oz  *Stoli* Vanilla Vodka

Fill the glass with orange juice. Garnish with orange slices.

---

**Bad Pick-Up Line**
I love your eyes, *both of them.*

---

## Vodka Key Lime

Tall glass, fill with ice.

    1 oz   *Smirnoff Lime Twist* Vodka
   1/2 oz  *Stoli* Vanilla Vodka

Fill the glass with sweet and sour. Garnish with lime slices.

## Vodka Key Lime Pie

Tall glass, fill with ice.

    1 oz   *Smirnoff Lime Twist* Vodka
   1/2 oz  *Stoli* Vanilla Vodka
   1/2 oz  Butterscotch Schnapps

Fill the glass with sweet and sour. Garnish with lime slices.

## Vodka Lemon Meringue

Tall glass, fill with ice.

   1/2 oz  *Absolut Citron* Vodka
   1/2 oz  *Absolut* Vanilla Vodka

Fill the glass with Sweet and Sour. Garnish with lemon slices coated in sugar.

## Vodka Lemon Meringue Pie

Tall glass, fill with ice.

   1/2 oz  *Absolut Citron* Vodka
   1/4 oz  *Absolut* Vanilla Vodka
   1/4 oz  Butterscotch Schnapps

Fill the glass with Sweet and Sour. Garnish with lemon slices.

# Whiskey Drinks

## Highball

Bucket glass, fill with ice.

1 oz　Bourbon

Fill the glass with Ginger Ale.

## Hot Whiskey Toddy

Large coffee cup, warmed.

1 oz　Whiskey
1/2 oz　Honey

Fill the cup with hot water. A tea bag may be added. Serve with lemon slices.

## Old Fashioned

Bucket glass.

　　　　1　Sugar cube
2 Dashes　Bitters
　　　　1　Orange slice
　　3-4　Cherries
　1 oz　*Jim Beam* Bourbon

Muddle (mush) the sugar, Bitters, orange slice and cherries together. Fill the glass with ice, add the bourbon, than fill the rest of the way with club soda. Garnish with cherries.

## Presbyterian (Press)

Bucket glass, fill with ice.

1 oz   Bourbon

Fill the glass with equal mix of Ginger Ale or 7-Up, and club soda.

---

A Presbyterian is commonly called a "Press," and can be made with different liquors, for example a Vodka Press or a Whiskey Press.

---

## Rusty Nail

Rocks glass, fill with ice.

1-1/2 oz   Scotch
1/2 oz   *Drambuie*

## Scotch and Soda

Bucket glass, fill with ice.

1 oz   Scotch

Fill the glass with club soda.

---

The ending "soda" means soda water or club soda is the mixer. Any hard liquor can be mixed with soda, for example, whiskey and soda, vodka and soda, or brandy and soda

Some cities, particularly on the East Coast, refer to cola (Coke) as "soda." When mixing drinks, soda refers to SODA WATER or CLUB SODA. When in doubt, ask your customer which one they mean.

---

# 7 and 7 (7/7)
Bucket glass, fill with ice.

    1 oz   ***Seagram's 7*** Whisky

Fill the glass with 7-Up.

The ending "7" means 7-Up is the mixer. Any hard liquor can be mixed with 7-Up' such as whiskey and 7, or vodka and 7.

# Silky Scotch
Rocks glass, fill with ice.

    1-1/2 oz   Scotch
    1/2 oz   ***Drambuie Sylk Cream***

# Whiskey Sour
Bucket glass, fill with ice.

    1 oz   Whiskey

Fill the glass with Sweet and Sour. Garnish with a cherry.

---

A man walks into a bar with a slab of concrete under his arm. He says to the bartender, "I'd like one for me, and one for the road."

# Lemonades and Iced Teas

## Black Opal

Tall glass, fill with ice.

| | |
|---|---|
| 1/2 oz | Vodka |
| 1/2 oz | Rum |
| 1/2 oz | Triple Sec |
| 1/2 oz | Gin |
| 2 oz | Sweet and Sour |

Nearly fill the glass with 7-Up. Top with 1/2 oz **Chambord.** Garnish with lemon slices.

## Blue Lemonade

Tall glass, fill with ice.

| | |
|---|---|
| 1/2 oz | Vodka |
| 1/2 oz | Rum |
| 1/2 oz | Blue *Curacao* |
| 1/2 oz | Gin |
| 2 oz | Sweet and Sour |

Fill the glass with 7-Up. Garnish with lemon slices.

The word "electric" means 1/2-ounce of tequila is floated on top of the drink

# Electric Lemonade
Tall glass, fill with ice.

1/2 oz   Vodka
1/2 oz   Rum
1/2 oz   Triple Sec
1/2 oz   Gin
2 oz   Sweet and Sour

Nearly fill the glass with 7-Up. Top with 1/2-oz tequila. Garnish with lemon slices.

# Hawaiian Dance Music
Tall glass, fill with ice.

1/2 oz   Vodka
1/2 oz   Rum
1/2 oz   Triple Sec
1/2 oz   Gin
2 oz   Sweet and Sour

Nearly fill the glass with 7-Up. Top with 1/2 oz *Midori.* Garnish with lime slices.

# Lemonade
Tall glass, fill with ice.

1/2 oz   Vodka
1/2 oz   Rum
1/2 oz   Triple Sec
1/2 oz   Gin
2 oz   Sweet and Sour

Fill the glass with 7-up. Garnish with lemon slices.

## Lynchburg Lemonade

Tall glass, fill with ice.

1 oz   ***Jack Daniel's*** Whiskey
1/2 oz   Triple Sec
1 oz   Sweet and Sour

Fill the glass with 7-Up. Garnish with lemon slices.

## Blackberry Iced Tea

Tall glass, fill with ice.

1/2 oz   Vodka
1/2 oz   Rum
1/2 oz   Triple Sec
1/2 oz   Gin
1/2 oz   ***Chambord***
1 oz   Sweet and Sour

Fill the glass with Coke. Garnish with lemon slices.

## *Electric* Long Island Iced Tea

Tall glass, fill with ice.

1/2 oz   Vodka
1/2 oz   Rum
1/2 oz   Triple Sec
1/2 oz   Gin
2 oz   Sweet and Sour

Nearly fill the glass with Coke. Top with 1/2 oz tequila. Garnish with lemon slices.

## Florida Iced Tea

Tall glass, fill with ice.

| | |
|---|---|
| 1/2 oz | Vodka |
| 1/2 oz | Rum |
| 1/2 oz | Triple Sec |
| 1/2 oz | Gin |
| 2 oz | Sweet and Sour |

Fill the glass with orange juice. Garnish with lemon slices.

## Green Apple Iced Tea

Tall glass, fill with ice.

| | |
|---|---|
| 1/2 oz | Vodka |
| 1/2 oz | Rum |
| 1/2 oz | Triple Sec |
| 1/2 oz | Gin |
| 1/2 oz | Apple Schnapps |
| 1 oz | Sweet and Sour |

Fill the glass with Coke. Garnish with lemon slices.

## Long Beach Iced Tea

Tall glass, fill with ice.

| | |
|---|---|
| 1/2 oz | Vodka |
| 1/2 oz | Rum |
| 1/2 oz | Triple Sec |
| 1/2 oz | Gin |
| 2 oz | Sweet and Sour |

Fill the glass with cranberry juice. Garnish with lemon slices.

# Long Island Iced Tea

Tall glass, fill with ice.

|        |              |
|--------|--------------|
| 1/2 oz | Vodka        |
| 1/2 oz | Rum          |
| 1/2 oz | Triple Sec   |
| 1/2 oz | Gin          |
| 2 oz   | Sweet and Sour |

Fill the glass with Coke. Garnish with lemon slices.

# Manhattan Iced Tea

Tall glass, fill with ice.

|        |                        |
|--------|------------------------|
| 1/2 oz | *Maker's Mark* Bourbon |
| 1/2 oz | Scotch                 |
| 1/2 oz | Triple Sec             |
| 1/2 oz | Tequila                |
| 1 oz   | Sweet and Sour         |

Fill the glass with Coke. Garnish with lemon slices.

# *Malibu* Melon Iced Tea

Tall glass, fill with ice.

|        |                |
|--------|----------------|
| 3/4 oz | Vodka          |
| 3/4 oz | *Malibu* Rum   |
| 1/2 oz | Triple Sec     |
| 1/2 oz | *Midori*       |
| 1 oz   | Sweet and Sour |

Fill the glass with Coke. Garnish with cherries.

# Peach Iced Tea
Tall glass, fill with ice.

| | |
|---|---|
| 1/2 oz | Vodka |
| 1/2 oz | Rum |
| 1/2 oz | Triple Sec |
| 1/2 oz | Gin |
| 1/2 oz | Peach Schnapps |
| 1 oz | Sweet and Sour |

Fill the glass with Coke. Garnish with peach slices.

# Pineapple-Coconut Iced Tea
Tall glass, fill with ice.

| | |
|---|---|
| 1/2 oz | *Malibu* Rum |
| 1/2 oz | Pineapple Rum |
| 1/2 oz | Triple Sec |
| 1/2 oz | Vodka |
| 2 oz | Piña Colada syrup or mix |
| 1 oz | Sweet and Sour |

Fill the glass with pineapple juice. Garnish with cherries.

# Raspberry Iced Tea
Tall glass, fill with ice.

| | |
|---|---|
| 1/2 oz | *Smirnoff Raspberry Twist* |
| 1/2 oz | Rum |
| 1/2 oz | Triple Sec |
| 1/2 oz | Gin |
| 1/2 oz | *RazzmaTazz* Raspberry Liqueur |
| 1 oz | Sweet and Sour |

Fill the glass with Coke. Garnish with cherries.

# Margaritas

## Basic Margarita

Bucket glass, salted rim, fill with ice.

**OR**

Mix with ice in a blender, and serve in a large margarita glass with a salted rim.

|        |                  |
|--------|------------------|
| 1 oz   | Tequila          |
| 1/2 oz | Triple Sec       |
| 1/4 oz | Rose's Lime Juice |
| 2 oz   | Sweet and Sour   |

Garnish with lime slices.

## Blackberry-Banana Margarita

Bucket glass, sugared rim, fill with ice.

**OR**

Mix with ice in a blender, and serve in a large margarita glass with a sugared rim.

|           |                            |
|-----------|----------------------------|
| 1 oz      | Tequila                    |
| 1/2 oz    | Triple Sec                 |
| 1/4 oz    | Rose's Lime Juice          |
| 1-1/2 cup | Fresh blackberries & bananas |
| 1/4 oz    | Blackberry flavored syrup  |
| 1/4 oz    | Banana flavored syrup      |
| 2 oz      | Sweet and Sour             |

Garnish with banana slices.

Margaritas can be made with a variety of fruits and berries. Flavored syrups, such as coconut or tropical fruit, can add an exotic twist. Piña Colada or Mai Tai syrup can also be used.

By substituting *rum* for the tequila and *deleting the Triple Sec*, the same recipes can be used to make wonderful daiquiris.

For virgin margaritas, use non-alcoholic Triple Sec, and add a little extra flavored syrup. You will love the results.

## Blue Margarita

Bucket glass, salted rim, fill with ice.
**OR**
Mix with ice in a blender, and serve in a large margarita glass with a salted rim.

| | |
|---|---|
| 1 oz | Tequila |
| 1/2 oz | Blue *Curacao* |
| 1/4 oz | Rose's Lime Juice |
| 2 oz | Sweet and Sour |

Garnish with lime slices.

*Curacao* is an orange flavored liqueur from the Island of Curacao. *Curacao* comes in a variety of fun colors and can be substituted for Triple Sec to create wild looking drinks such as bright green margaritas and brilliant purple lemonades.

When you see an exotic drink that is a dark blue, or turquoise, chances are very good that it was made using blue *Curacao*.

## Cadillac Margarita

Bucket glass, salted rim, fill with ice.
* * *OR* * *
Mix with ice in a blender, and serve in a large margarita glass with a salted rim.

| | |
|---|---|
| 1 oz | *Jose Cuervo* Gold Tequila |
| 1/2 oz | *Grand Marnier* |
| 1/4 oz | Rose's Lime Juice |
| 2 oz | Sweet and Sour |

Garnish with lime slices.

## Gold Margarita

Bucket glass, salted rim, fill with ice.
* * *OR* * *
Mix with ice in a blender, and serve in a large margarita glass with a salted rim.

| | |
|---|---|
| 1 oz | *Jose Cuervo* Gold Tequila |
| 1/2 oz | Triple Sec |
| 1/4 oz | Rose's Lime Juice |
| 2 oz | Sweet and Sour |

Garnish with lime slices.

## *HYPNOTIQ* Margarita

Bucket glass, salted rim, fill with ice.
* * *OR* * *
Mix with ice in a blender, and serve in a large margarita glass with a salted rim.

| | |
|---|---|
| 1 oz | *Jose Cuervo* Gold Tequila |
| 2 oz | *HYPNOTIQ* |
| 1/4 oz | Rose's Lime Juice |
| 2 oz | Sweet and Sour |

Garnish with lime slices.

# Kiwi Margarita

Bucket glass, sugared rim, fill with ice.
*\* OR \**
Mix with ice in a blender, and serve in a large margarita glass
with a sugared rim.

| | |
|---|---|
| 1 oz | Tequila |
| 1/2 oz | Triple Sec or *Cointreau* |
| 1/4 oz | Rose's Lime Juice |
| 2 oz | Kiwi Puree **or** |
| 1/2 cup | Fresh kiwis - blended |
| 1/2 oz | Kiwi flavored syrup |
| 2 oz | Sweet and Sour |

Garnish with kiwi or strawberry slices.

# Mango-Apricot Margarita

Bucket glass, sugared rim, fill with ice.
*\* OR \**
Mix with ice in a blender, and serve in a large margarita glass
with a sugared rim.

| | |
|---|---|
| 1 oz | Tequila |
| 1/2 oz | Triple Sec |
| 1/4 oz | Rose's Lime Juice |
| 1/2 cup | Fresh mango - blended |
| 1/2 cup | Fresh apricots - blended |
| 1/2 oz | Peach flavored syrup |
| 1/2 oz | Mango or Mai-Tai flavored syrup |
| 2 oz | Sweet and Sour |

Garnish with cherries or apricot slices.

# Peach Margarita

Bucket glass, sugared rim, fill with ice.
**\* \* *OR* \* \***
Mix with ice in a blender, and serve in a large margarita glass with a sugared rim.

| | |
|---|---|
| 1 oz | Tequila |
| 1/2 oz | Triple Sec |
| 1/4 oz | Rose's Lime Juice |
| 2 oz | Peach puree **or** |
| 1/2 cup | Fresh peaches - blended |
| 1/2 oz | Peach flavored syrup |
| 2 oz | Sweet and Sour |

Garnish with peach slices.

# Raspberry Margarita

Bucket glass, sugared rim, fill with ice.
**\* \* *OR* \* \***
Mix with ice in a blender, and serve in a large margarita glass with a sugared rim.

| | |
|---|---|
| 1 oz | Tequila |
| 1/2 oz | Triple Sec |
| 1/4 oz | Rose's Lime Juice |
| 1/2 cup | Fresh raspberries |
| 1/2 oz | Raspberry flavored syrup |
| 2 oz | Sweet and Sour |

Garnish with raspberries.

---

Use club soda or soda water to help remove wine stains from clothing or furniture.

# Strawberry Margarita

Bucket glass, sugared rim, fill with ice.
*  * OR  * *
Mix with ice in a blender, and serve in a large margarita glass
with a sugared rim.

| | |
|---|---|
| 1 oz | Tequila |
| 1/2 oz | Triple Sec or *Cointreau* |
| 1/4 oz | Rose's Lime Juice |
| 2 oz | Strawberry puree **or** |
| 1/2 cup | Fresh strawberries - blended |
| 1/2 oz | Strawberry flavored syrup |
| 2 oz | Sweet and Sour |

Garnish with strawberry slices.

# Watermelon Margarita

Bucket glass, sugared rim, fill with ice.
*  * OR  * *
Mix with ice in a blender, and serve in a large margarita glass
with a sugared rim.

| | |
|---|---|
| 1 oz | Watermelon Tequila |
| 1/4 cup | Watermelon squares (seeded) |
| 1/2 oz | Triple Sec |
| 1/2 oz | Watermelon flavored syrup |
| 1/4 oz | Rose's Lime Juice |
| 2 oz | Sweet and Sour |

Garnish with watermelon wedges or lime slices.

---

I would make a terrible politician. I can never
remember a person's name. But tell me what they drink,
and I will know exactly whom you are talking about.

---

# Martinis and Manhattans

Martinis and Gibsons are made with gin, vodka, or a combination of gin and vodka.

Manhattans are traditionally made with bourbon, but many times other whiskeys are used.

A Manhattan made with <u>scotch</u> is often called a <u>Rob Roy</u>.

Call names for the liquors may be used:

- *Johnny Walker* Rob Roy
- *Bushmill's* Manhattan
- *Tanqueray* Martini
- *Gray Goose* Gibson
- *Absolut* Martini

- **<u>On the Rocks</u>** -Serve in a rocks glass filled with ice. Add the Vermouth, than add the main liquor.

- **<u>Straight Up</u>** - Serve in a chilled martini glass, no ice. In a mixing glass add 1 cup of ice and the Vermouth. Next, add the main liquor. Shake or stir, and strain into a chilled martini glass.

- The more "dry" the martini, the <u>less</u> Dry Vermouth is used.

- For a "dirty martini," add about 1/4 oz olive juice (from the green olives) to the drink after mixing, before serving.

- A Gibson is the same as a Martini with a pearl onion instead of an olive.

## Martini
Martini glass, chilled. Shake with ice and strain:

4-6 Drops **DRY** Vermouth
2 oz Gin or Vodka

Garnish with a green olive on a spear or pick.

*swirl + toss*

## Dry Martini
Martini glass, chilled. Shake with ice and strain:

2-4 Drops **DRY** Vermouth
2 oz Gin or Vodka

Garnish with a green olive on a spear or pick.

*in-out*

## Extra Dry Martini
Martini glass, chilled. Shake with ice and strain:

1-2 Drops **DRY** Vermouth
2 oz Gin or Vodka

Garnish with a green olive on a spear or pick.

*spoon*

## Extra Extra Dry Martini
Martini glass, chilled. Shake with ice and strain:

0-1 Drops **DRY** Vermouth
2 oz Gin or Vodka

Garnish with a green olive on a spear or pick.

*'wave + passing'*

## Gibson
Martini glass, chilled. Shake with ice and strain:

4-6 Drops **DRY** Vermouth
2 oz Gin or Vodka

Garnish with a pearl onion on a spear or pick.

*swirl + toss*

## Dry Gibson

Martini glass, chilled. Shake with ice and strain:

2-4 Drops **DRY** Vermouth

2 oz Gin or Vodka

Garnish with a pearl onion on a spear or pick.

*in - out*

## Extra Dry Gibson

Martini glass, chilled. Shake with ice and strain:

1-2 Drops **DRY** Vermouth

2 oz Gin or Vodka

Garnish with a pearl onion on a spear or pick.

*spoon*

## Extra Extra Dry Gibson

Martini glass, chilled. Shake with ice and strain:

0-1 Drops **DRY** Vermouth

2 oz Gin or Vodka

Garnish with a pearl onion on a spear or pick.

*wave + passing*

## Manhattan

Martini glass, chilled. Shake with ice and strain:

1/4 oz **SWEET** Vermouth

2 oz Bourbon

Garnish with a cherry.

## Dry Manhattan

Martini glass, chilled. Shake with ice and strain:

1/4 oz **DRY** Vermouth

2 oz Bourbon

Garnish with a green olive on a spear or pick.

## Perfect Manhattan

Martini glass, chilled. Shake with ice and strain:

1/8 oz   **SWEET** Vermouth

1/8 oz   **DRY** Vermouth

2 oz   Bourbon

Garnish with a lemon twist.

# Exotic Martinis

## Adios Mother Pucker-Tini

Martini or cocktail glass, chilled. Shake with ice and strain:

1/4 oz   *Watermelon Puckers*

1/4 oz   *Peach Puckers*

1/4 oz   *Sour Apple Puckers*

1 oz   Vodka

1/2 oz   7-Up

1/2 oz   Club soda

** This drink can foam up very quickly. Shake it gently or you will be wearing it! Garnish with cherries.

## Apple-Tini

Martini or cocktail glass, chilled. Shake with ice and strain:

1-1/2 oz   Vodka

1-1/2 oz   Rose's Cocktail Infusion's Sour Apple

Garnish with cherries.

*different Puckers = different drinks*

## Apple-Tini 2

Martini or cocktail glass, chilled. Shake with ice and strain:

*more common than #1*

1 oz　　Vodka
1/2 oz　*Apple Puckers*
~~1 oz~~　Sweet and Sour
2 oz

Garnish with cherries.

} *Same drink in bucket glass = Jolly Rancher over ice*

## Apple-ishious-Tini

Martini or cocktail glass, chilled. Shake with ice and strain:

1 oz　　Vanilla Vodka
1/2 oz　*Apple Puckers*
1 oz　　Pineapple juice

Garnish with cherries.

## Apple-ini Creamy-Tini

Martini or cocktail glass, chilled. Shake with ice and strain:

1-1/2 oz　　Vanilla Vodka
1-1/2 oz　　Rose's Cocktail Infusion's Sour Apple

Garnish with cherries.

## Berry-Tini

Martini or cocktail glass, chilled. Shake with ice and strain:

1 oz　　Raspberry Vodka
1/2 oz　Chambord
1 oz　　Sweet and Sour

Garnish with cherries.

## Between the Sheets

Martini or cocktail glass, chilled. Shake with ice and strain:

| | |
|---|---|
| 1/2 oz | Triple Sec |
| 1/2 oz | Rum |
| 1/2 oz | Brandy |
| 2 oz | Sweet and Sour |

## Blue Hypno Goose Martini

Martini or cocktail glass, chilled. Shake with ice and strain:

| | |
|---|---|
| 2 oz | *HPNOTIQ* |
| 1 oz | *Gray Goose* Vodka |
| Splash | Pineapple juice |

Garnish with a pineapple wedge.

## Blue Hawaiian Martini

Martini or cocktail glass, chilled. Shake with ice and strain:

| | |
|---|---|
| 2 oz | *Grey Goose* Vodka |
| 1 oz | Rose's Cocktail Infusion's Blue Raspberry |
| 1 oz | Rose's Cocktail Infusion's Sour Apple |

Garnish with a lemon twist and cherries.

## Blue Raspberry Martini

Martini or cocktail glass, chilled. Shake with ice and strain:

| | |
|---|---|
| 1-1/2 oz | Vodka |
| 1-1/2 oz | Rose's Cocktail Infusion's Blue Raspberry |

Garnish with cherries.

## Blue Raspberry Tini Twist

Martini or cocktail glass, chilled. Shake with ice and strain:

1-1/2 oz   *Stoli Limon* Vodka
1-1/2 oz   Rose's Cocktail Infusion's Blue
             Raspberry

Garnish with a lemon twist and cherries.

## Caramel Apple-Tini

Martini or cocktail glass, chilled, sugared rim. Shake with ice and strain:

3/4 oz   Vodka
1/2 oz   *Apple Puckers*
1/2 oz   *Tuaca* or Butterscotch Schnapps
1/4 oz   Triple Sec
Splash   Sweet and Sour

Garnish with apple slices or cherries.

## Cherry Cordial Martini

Martini or cocktail glass, chilled. Layer:

1 oz   *Kahlua*
1 oz   Cherry Brandy
1 oz   Cream

Garnish with whipped cream and grenadine.

---

Many recipes can be converted to martinis by simply reducing the increments of the ingredients so they will fit into the class. Shake and strain, or serve layered, no ice.

# Chocolate Decadence Martini
Martini or cocktail glass, chilled. Layer:

1/2 oz  *Kahlua*
1/2 oz  *Bailey's* Irish Cream
1 oz    VanillaVodka

Garnish with *Godiva Dark Chocolate* liqueur.

# Chocolate Strawberry-Tini
Martini or cocktail glass, chilled. Layer:

1/2 oz  *Bailey's* Irish Cream
1/2 oz  *Godiva Dark Chocolate* Liqueur
1 oz    Strawberry Vodka

Garnish with strawberries, drizzle with dark chocolate syrup.

# Cosmopolitan
Martini or cocktail glass, chilled. Shake with ice and strain:

1-1/2 oz  Vodka
1/2 oz    Rose's Lime Juice
1/2 oz    Cranberry juice

Garnish with lime slices, or a lemon twist.

# Cosmopolitan 2
Martini or cocktail glass, chilled. Shake with ice and strain:

1 oz    Vodka
1/2 oz  Amaretto
1/2 oz  Cranberry juice

Garnish with lemon slices, or a lemon twist.

## Cosmopolitan 3

Martini or cocktail glass, chilled. Shake with ice and strain:

    1 oz    Vodka
    1/2 oz    Peach Schnapps
    1/2 oz    Cranberry juice

Garnish with lemon slices, or a lemon twist.

## Cosmopolitan 4

Martini or cocktail glass, chilled. Shake with ice and strain:

    1 oz    Vodka
    1/2 oz    Cherry Brandy
    1/2 oz    Cranberry juice

Garnish with cherries and a lemon twist.

## Cosmopolitan 5

Martini or cocktail glass, chilled. Shake with ice and strain:

    1-1/2 oz    Vodka
    1-1/2 oz    Rose's Cocktail Infusion's
                Cranberry Twist

Garnish with lemon slices, or a lemon twist.

## Cosmopolitan - *HYPNOTIQ*

Martini or cocktail glass, chilled. Shake with ice and strain:

    1 oz    *HYPNOTIQ*
    1/2 oz    Roses's Lime Juice
    1/2 oz    Cranberry juice

Garnish with a lime twist.

## Cosmopolitan - White

Martini or cocktail glass, chilled. Shake with ice and strain:

1 oz Vodka
1/2 oz Roses's Lime Juice
1/2 oz White Cranberry juice

Garnish with a lime twist.

## Cosmopolitan Orange Twist

Martini or cocktail glass, chilled. Shake with ice and strain:

1-1/2 oz *Absolut Mandarin* Vodka
1-1/2 oz Rose's Cocktail Infusion's
Cranberry Twist

Garnish with lemon slices, or a lemon twist.

## Cream Dream-a-Tini

Martini or cocktail glass, chilled. Layer:

1/2 oz *Bailey's* Irish Cream
1/2 oz Crème de Cacao
1 oz Raspberry Vodka
1/2 oz *Chambord*

Garnish with strawberries, drizzle with Crème de Cacao.

## Florida Peach Martini

Martini or cocktail glass, chilled. Shake with ice and strain:

1 oz Mango Vodka
1/2 oz Peach Schnapps
1 oz Orange juice

Garnish with peaches.

# Grape-Tini

Martini or cocktail glass, chilled. Shake with ice and strain:

    1 oz   Vodka
    1/2 oz  ***Grape Puckers***
    1 oz   Sweet and Sour

Garnish with cherries.

# Grape-Berry Martini

Martini or cocktail glass, chilled. Shake with ice and strain:

    1 oz  ***Stoli Raspberry*** Vodka
    1/2 oz  ***Raspberry Puckers***
    1 oz  Rose's Cocktail Infusion's
          Blue Raspberry

Garnish with cherries.

# Heated Hooters Martini

Martini or cocktail glass, chilled. Layer:

    2 oz  ***Bailey's*** Irish Cream (bottom)
    1/2 oz  Butterscotch Schnapps
    1/2 oz  ***Goldschlager***

Garnish with strawberries, top with drops of grenadine.

# *HPNOTIQ* Martini

Martini or cocktail glass, chilled. Shake with ice and strain:

    1-1/2 oz  ***HPNOTIQ***
    1 oz  Vodka
    Splash  Lemon juice

Garnish with a lemon twist.

## Lemon Drop Martini

Martini or cocktail glass, chilled. Sugared rim.
Shake with ice and strain:

| | |
|---|---|
| 1 oz | Vodka |
| 1/2 oz | Triple Sec |
| 1/2 oz | Lemon juice |

Garnish with lemon slices covered in sugar.

## Mango-Tango-Tini

Martini or cocktail glass, chilled. Shake with ice and strain:

| | |
|---|---|
| 1 oz | Mango Vodka |
| 1/2 oz | *Cointreau* |
| 1 oz | Cranberry juice |

Garnish with cherries.

## Mango-Meltdown-Tini

Martini or cocktail glass, chilled. Shake with ice and strain:

| | |
|---|---|
| 1 oz | Mango Vodka |
| 1/2 oz | *Peach Puckers* |
| 1 oz | Mango juice |

Garnish with cherries.

## Peach-Tini

Martini or cocktail glass, chilled. Shake with ice and strain:

| | |
|---|---|
| 1 oz | Vanilla Vodka |
| 1/2 oz | Peach Schnapps |
| 1 oz | Sweet and Sour |

Garnish with cherries.

# Peach-Tini 2

Martini or cocktail glass, chilled. Shake with ice and strain:

>  1 oz   Vanilla Vodka
> 1/2 oz   ***Peach Puckers***
>  1 oz   Sweet and Sour

Garnish with cherries.

# Purple Gecko Martini

Martini or cocktail glass, chilled. Shake with ice and strain:

> 2 oz   ***Grey Goose*** Vodka
> 1 oz   Rose's Cocktail Infusion's Blue Raspberry
> 1 oz   Rose's Cocktail Infusion's Cranberry Twist

Garnish with a lemon twist and cherries.

# Raspberry Colada Martini

Martini or cocktail glass, chilled. Shake with ice and strain:

> 2 oz   ***Baja Luna*** Raspberry Tequila
> 1 oz   Piña Colada mix
> 1 oz   Cream

Garnish with whipped cream and grenadine.

# Southern Comfort Manhattan

Martini glass, chilled. Shake with ice and strain:

> 1/4 oz   **DRY** Vermouth
>  2 oz   ***Southern Comfort***

Garnish with a cherry.

# Tennessee Slammer

Martini or cocktail glass, chilled.

|        |                       |
|--------|-----------------------|
| 1/4 oz | *Jack Daniel's* Whiskey |
| 1/4 oz | *Yukon Jack* Whiskey  |
| 1/4 oz | *Southern Comfort*    |
| 1/4 oz | *Wild Turkey* Bourbon |
| 1/2 oz | Cranberry juice       |
| 1/2 oz | Pineapple juice       |
| Splash | Grenadine             |

# Toasted Peaches

Martini or cocktail glass, chilled. Layer:

|      |               |
|------|---------------|
| 1 oz | *Kahlua*      |
| 2 oz | Cream         |
| 1 oz | Peach Schnapps |

Garnish with whipped cream and *Kahlua*.

# Toasted Raspberries

Martini or cocktail glass, chilled. Layer:

|      |                          |
|------|--------------------------|
| 1 oz | *Kahlua*                 |
| 1 oz | *Baja Luna* Raspberry Tequila |
| 2 oz | Cream                    |

Garnish with whipped cream and grenadine.

# Very Blue Berry Martini

Martini or cocktail glass, chilled. Shake with ice and strain:

|      |                                         |
|------|-----------------------------------------|
| 2 oz | *Stoli Strawberry* Vodka                |
| 1 oz | Rose's Cocktail Infusion's Blue Raspberry |

Garnish with strawberries.

# Famous Drinks of Our Favorite Spy

## "A vodka martini. Shaken, not stirred."
*James Bond 007*

### 007 Vodka Martini

This cocktail was made famous in the MGM/UA movie, **Dr. No**, starring Sean Connery.

Champagne goblet, chilled. Shake with ice and strain:

| | |
|---|---|
| 1-1/2 oz | **Gordon's** Gin |
| 1/2 oz | Vodka |
| 1/4 oz | **Kina Lillet** Dry Vermouth |

Garnish with a thin slice of lemon peel.

### Mint Julep

The Mint Julep has been a popular drink of the Deep South for over 200 years. MGM/UA and Sean Connery made it famous in the 1964 movie, **Goldfinger.**

Collins glass, 1/2 fill with ice.

| | |
|---|---|
| 2 oz | Bourbon |
| 5 or 6 | Fresh mint leaves |
| 1/2 oz | Simple Syrup |

Muddle (mash) the ice, mint leaves, Simple Syrup and half the bourbon together. Next, add the rest of the bourbon and fill the glass with ice. Garnish with fresh mint leaves.

# Mojito

This famous drink is from the 2002 MGM/UA movie, *Die Another Day*, starring Pierce Brosnan.

Collins glass, fill with ice.

    1 oz   Light Rum
  1/2 tsp   Sugar

Squeeze the juice from half a lime into the drink then fill the glass with soda water. Garnish with Mojito Mint sprigs.

## Sources:

"Drink Like 007," *MI6 – The Home of 007*, 26th November 2002, <http://www.mi6.co.uk/sections/ articles/drink_ like_007.php3?t =&s=articles>, (5 May 2004).
**If you are a James Bond fan, you absolutely must see this site.**

"Make Mine a 007 – The James Bond Films," *The Minister of Martinis*, 2002, <http://home.earthlink.net/ ~atomic_rom/007/films.htm>, (5 May 2004).

"Why did James Bond want his martinis shaken, not stirred?," *The Straight Dope*, 28-Nov-2000, <http://www.straightdope.com/ mailbag/mmartini.html>, (5 May 2004).

---

### Bad Pick-Up Line

Man: "You must have a mirror in your pocket."
Waitress: "What are you talking about?"
Man: "Because I see myself in your pants!"

# Coffee, Tea, and Hot Chocolate Drinks

## Almond Excellence

Large coffee cup, warmed.

    1 oz   Amaretto
    1 Tbs  Honey

Fill the cup with hot tea. Garnish with a lemon wedge.

## Almond Joyous

Large coffee cup, warmed.

    3/4 oz  Crème de Cacao
    3/4 oz  Amaretto

Fill the cup with hot chocolate. Garnish with whipped cream.

## *Bailey's* Coffee

Large coffee cup, warmed. 1/2 fill with <u>fresh,</u> hot coffee.

    1-1/2 oz  *Bailey's* Irish Cream

Fill the cup with coffee. Garnish with whipped cream.

## *Bailey's* 'n Brandy Coffee

Large coffee cup, warmed. 1/2 fill with <u>fresh,</u> hot coffee.

    1 oz  *Bailey's* Irish Cream
    1 oz  Brandy

Fill the cup with coffee. Garnish with whipped cream.

## Candlelight Coffee
Large coffee cup, warmed.

1/2 oz   Peach Schnapps
1/2 oz   Crème de Noyaux (Almond)
1 oz   *Bacardi* 151 Rum

Fill the mug with coffee. Garnish with whipped cream.

## Chocolate Caramel Apples
Large coffee cup, warmed.

1/2 oz   Apple Schnapps (not *Puckers*)
1/2 oz   Butterscotch Schnapps

Fill the cup with hot chocolate. Garnish with whipped cream.

## Chocolate Caramel Nudge
Large coffee cup, warmed.

1/2 oz   *Kahlua*
1/2 oz   Butterscotch Schnapps

Fill the cup with hot chocolate. Garnish with whipped cream.

## Chocolate Covered Apricots
Large coffee cup, warmed.

1 oz   Apricot Brandy

Fill the cup with hot chocolate. Garnish with whipped cream.
(A personal favorite.)

## Coffee Bitch

Large coffee cup, warmed. 1/2 fill with <u>fresh</u>, hot coffee.

1/2 oz   ***Bailey's*** Irish Cream
1/2 oz   ***Yukon Jack*** Whiskey

Fill the cup with coffee. Garnish with whipped cream.

## Coffee Calypso

Large coffee cup, warmed. 1/2 fill with <u>fresh</u>, hot coffee.

1/2 oz   ***Kahlua***
1/2 oz   Rum
1/2 tsp.   Sugar

Fill the cup with coffee. Garnish with whipped cream.

## French Coffee

Large coffee cup, warmed.

1/2 oz   ***Grand Marnier***
1/2 oz   Cognac or Brandy

Fill the cup with fresh, hot coffee. Garnish with whipped cream.

## Grasshopper Warm-up

Large coffee cup, warmed.

3/4 oz   Crème de Cacao
3/4 oz   Crème de Menthe

Fill the cup with hot chocolate. Garnish with whipped cream.

---

Stale coffee can cause Irish Cream to curdle.

## Irish Coffee

Large coffee cup, warmed.

   1 oz    Irish Whiskey

Fill the cup with fresh, hot coffee. Add sugar if requested. Garnish with whipped cream.

## Italian Coffee

Large coffee cup, warmed.

   1 oz    Amaretto

Fill the cup with fresh, hot coffee. Garnish with whipped cream.

## Jamaican Coffee

Large coffee cup, warmed. 1/2 fill with <u>fresh</u>, hot coffee.

   1/2-oz    *Bailey's* Irish Cream
   1/2 oz    *Myers'* Rum

Fill the cup with coffee.

## Kioki Calypso

Large coffee cup, warmed. 1/2 fill with <u>fresh</u>, hot coffee.

   1/2 oz    *Kahlua*
   1/2 oz    Brandy
   1/2 oz    **Brown** Crème de Cacao

Fill the cup with coffee. Garnish with whipped cream.

## Mexican Coffee

Large coffee cup, warmed. 1/2 fill with <u>fresh</u>, hot coffee.

    1 oz   *Kahlua*

Fill the cup with coffee. Garnish with whipped cream.

## Peach Tea Warm-up

Large coffee cup, warmed.

    3/4 oz   Peach Schnapps
    3/4 oz   Cognac

Fill the cup with hot peach tea. Garnish with a lemon wedge coated in sugar.

## Scottish Coffee

Large coffee cup, warmed.

    1/2 oz   Scotch
    1/2 oz   *Drambuie*

Fill the cup with coffee. Garnish with whipped cream.

## Scottish Tea

Large coffee cup, warmed.

    1 oz   Scotch
    1 Tbs.   Honey

Fill the cup with hot tea. Garnish with a lemon wedge.

# Ski Lift

Large coffee cup, warmed.

1 oz   *Kahlua*
1/2 oz   Peppermint Schnapps

Fill the cup with coffee or hot chocolate. Garnish with whipped cream.

# Southern Hospitali-Tea

Large coffee cup, warmed.

1 oz   *Southern Comfort*
1 Tbs.   Honey

Fill the cup with hot tea. Garnish with a lemon wedge.

# Spanish Coffee

Large coffee cup, warmed.

1 oz   Tequila

Fill the cup with fresh, hot coffee. Garnish with whipped cream.

# Cream Drinks

## Almond Joyous

Cocktail glass, chilled, no ice. Shake with ice and strain:

1/2 oz   Amaretto
1/2 oz   **White** Crème de Cacao
2 oz   Cream

Garnish with shaved chocolate.

## Banshee

Cocktail glass, chilled, no ice. Shake with ice and strain:

1/2 oz   **White** Crème de Cacao
1/2 oz   Crème de Banana
2 oz   Cream

Garnish with whipped cream and drizzle with sliced bananas and/or shaved chocolate.

## Brandy Alexander

Cocktail glass, chilled, no ice. Shake with ice and strain:

1/2 oz   **Brown** Crème de Cacao
1/2 oz   Brandy
2 oz   Cream

Garnish with whipped cream and drizzle with Crème de Cacao or shaved chocolate.

# Chocolate Covered Strawberries

Bucket glass, fill with ice.

1 oz   *Kahlua*
1 oz   *Baja Rosa* Strawberry Tequila
2 oz   Cream

Garnish with whipped cream and drizzle with *Kahlua.*

# Chocolate Raspberries and Cream

Shaker glass, 1/3 filled with ice.

1 oz   *Kahlua*
1/2 oz   *Bailey's* Irish Cream
1 oz   *Baja Luna* Raspberry Tequila
1 oz   Cream

Fill the shaker glass to the top with whipped cream. Shake with ice and strain the combination into a chilled cocktail glass. Garnish with whipped cream drizzled with *Baja Luna.*

# Cricket

Cocktail glass, chilled, no ice. Shake with ice and strain:

1/2 oz   **Brown** Crème de Cacao
1/2 oz   **Green** Crème de Menthe
2 oz   Cream

Garnish with whipped cream and drizzle with Crème de Menthe and/or shaved chocolate.

---

### Pick Up Line "Hall of Fame"

If I told you that you have a great body, would you hold it against me?

# Dreamsickle
Bucket glass, fill with ice.

1 oz   Orange juice
1 oz   Amaretto

Fill the glass with cream

# Golden Cadillac
Cocktail glass, chilled, no ice. Shake with ice and strain:

1/2 oz   *Galliano*
1/2 oz   **White** Crème de Cacao
2 oz     Cream

Garnish with shaved chocolate.

# Golden Dream
Cocktail glass, chilled, no ice. Shake with ice and strain:

1/2 oz   *Galliano*
1/2 oz   Triple Sec
1/2 oz   Orange juice
2 oz     Cream

# Grasshopper
Cocktail glass, chilled, no ice. Shake with ice and strain:

1/2 oz   **White** Crème de Cacao
1/2 oz   **Green** Crème de Menthe
2 oz     Cream

Garnish with whipped cream and drizzle with Crème de Menthe and/or shaved chocolate.

# Peaches and Cream
Shaker glass, 1/3 filled with ice.

> 1/2 oz   *Stoli* Vanilla Vodka
> 1-1/2 oz   Peach Schnapps
> 1 oz   Cream

Fill the shaker glass to the top with whipped cream. Shake with ice and strain the combination into a chilled cocktail glass. Garnish with whipped cream, and drizzle with grenadine.

# Pink Lady
Cocktail glass, chilled, no ice. Shake with ice and strain:

> 1 oz   Gin
> 1/2 oz   Grenadine
> 2 oz   Cream

Garnish with grenadine.

---

The *Pink Lady* is a drink with some history behind it. During the early 1900's ladies of quality were not allowed to drink strong liquor. The closest they came was a little wine, or maybe a touch of brandy, "to settle their delicate nerves."

Taking matters into their own hands, the women of Boston convinced the local bartenders to create a special drink for them. The result was a pretty pink cocktail, which hid a full shot of 86 proof gin.

No self-respecting man would think of tasting the concoction, but the women left nothing to chance and either bribed or threatened the bartenders into submission. The secret was kept for nearly 20 years.

# Pink Squirrel

Cocktail glass, chilled, no ice. Shake with ice and strain:

| | |
|---|---|
| 1/2 oz | **White** Crème de Cacao |
| 1/2 oz | Crème de Noyaux (Almond) |
| 2 oz | Cream |

Garnish with whipped cream and grenadine.

# Toasted Almond

Bucket glass, fill with ice.

| | |
|---|---|
| 1 oz | *Kahlua* |
| 1 oz | Amaretto |
| 2 oz | Cream |

Garnish with whipped cream and *Kahlua*.

# Toasted Peaches

Bucket glass, fill with ice.

| | |
|---|---|
| 1 oz | *Kahlua* |
| 1 oz | Peach Schnapps |
| 2 oz | Cream |

Garnish with whipped cream and *Kahlua*.

# Toasted Raspberries

Bucket glass, fill with ice.

| | |
|---|---|
| 1 oz | *Kahlua* |
| 1 oz | *Baja Luna* Raspberry Tequila |
| 2 oz | Cream |

Garnish with whipped cream and grenadine.

```
┌─────────────────────────────────────────┐
│                                         │
│         Ice Cream Drinks                │
│     (Low Alcohol & Non-Alcoholic)       │
│                                         │
└─────────────────────────────────────────┘
```

# Ice Cream Drinks
## (Low Alcohol & Non-Alcoholic)

The flavored syrups I refer to in this chapter can be found at your local grocery store, or specialty kitchen and coffee supply. These are the same syrups used in making Italian sodas, specialty coffee and espresso drinks.

## Almond Joyous (Low Alcohol)
Blend and pour into a large cocktail glass.

| | |
|---|---|
| 2 scoops | Coconut ice cream |
| 1/3 cup | Ice |
| 2 oz | Cream |
| 1/2 oz | **White** Crème de Cacao |
| 1 oz | Coconut flavored syrup |
| 2 Tbs. | Crushed almonds |
| 2 Tbs. | Crushed coconut |

Garnish with whipped cream and shaved chocolate or dribble with chocolate syrup and grenadine.

---

### Fun Additions
Add Gummy Bears, miniature marshmallows, small gumdrops, jellybeans, or colorful candy sprinkles (the type used for making cookies).

---

## Almond Joyous (Non Alcoholic)
Blend and pour into a large cocktail glass.

| | |
|---|---|
| 2 scoops | Coconut ice cream |
| 1/3 cup | Ice |
| 2 oz | Cream |
| 1 oz | *Hershey's* Chocolate Syrup |
| 1 oz | Coconut flavored syrup |
| 2 Tbs. | Crushed coconut |
| 2 Tbs. | Crushed almonds |

Garnish with whipped cream, colorful candy sprinkles and a cherry. Drizzle with grenadine for a colorful red accent.

## Banshee (Low Alcohol)
Blend and pour into a large cocktail glass.

| | |
|---|---|
| 2 scoops | French Vanilla ice cream |
| 1/3 cup | Ice |
| 2 oz | Cream |
| 1/2 oz | Crème de Banana |
| 1/2 oz | *Hershey's* Chocolate Syrup |
| 1 | Peeled banana |

Garnish with whipped cream, cherries, banana slices, and shaved chocolate or miniature *Hershey's Kisses*. Drizzle with chocolate syrup.

---

Add strawberries and butterscotch topping
to make a Banana Split.

## Banshee   (Non Alcoholic)
Blend and pour into a large cocktail glass.

| | |
|---|---|
| 2 scoops | French Vanilla ice cream |
| 1/3 cup | Ice |
| 2 oz | Cream |
| 1 oz | Banana flavored syrup |
| 1/2 oz | *Hershey's* Chocolate Syrup |
| 1 | Peeled banana |

Garnish with whipped cream, cherries, banana slices, and chocolate syrup.

## Brandy Alexander   (Low Alcohol)
Blend and pour into a large cocktail glass.

| | |
|---|---|
| 2 scoops | French Vanilla ice cream |
| 1/3 cup | Ice |
| 2 oz | Cream |
| 1/2 oz | Brandy |
| 1/2 oz | *Hershey's* Chocolate Syrup |

Garnish with whipped cream, cherries and miniature *Hershey's Kisses.*

## Brandy Alexander   (Non Alcoholic)
Blend and pour into a large cocktail glass.

| | |
|---|---|
| 2 scoops | French Vanilla ice cream |
| 1/3 cup | Ice |
| 2 oz | Cream |
| 1 oz | Brandy flavored syrup |
| 1/2 oz | *Hershey's* Chocolate Syrup |

Garnish with whipped cream, cherries, and miniature *Hershey's Kisses*.

## Dreamsickle (Low Alcohol)
Blend and pour into a large cocktail glass.

| | |
|---|---|
| 2 scoops | French Vanilla ice cream |
| 1/3 cup | Ice |
| 2 oz | Cream |
| 1 oz | Orange flavored syrup |
| 1/2 oz | Amaretto |

Garnish with whipped cream.

## Dreamsickle (Non-Alcoholic)
Blend and pour into a large cocktail glass.

| | |
|---|---|
| 2 scoops | French Vanilla ice cream |
| 1/3 cup | Ice |
| 2 oz | Cream |
| 1 oz | Orange flavored syrup |
| 1/2 oz | Rum flavored syrup |

Garnish with whipped cream.

## Grasshopper (Low Alcohol)
Blend and pour into a large cocktail glass.

| | |
|---|---|
| 2 scoops | French Vanilla or mint ice cream |
| 1/3 cup | Ice |
| 2 oz | Cream |
| 1/2 oz | **Green** Crème de Menthe |
| 1/2 oz | *Hershey's* Chocolate Syrup |

Add a couple of drops of green food coloring if needed. Garnish with whipped cream, cherries, miniature *Hershey's Kisses* or *Andie's* candies. Drizzle with chocolate syrup.

# Grasshopper (Non Alcoholic)

Blend and pour into a large cocktail glass.

| | |
|---|---|
| 2 scoops | Chocolate mint ice cream |
| 1/3 cup | Ice |
| 2 oz | Cream |
| 1 oz | Chocolate mint flavored syrup |
| 1/2 oz | *Hershey's* Chocolate Syrup |

Garnish with whipped cream, cherries and *Andie's* candies. Drizzle with chocolate syrup.

> A grasshopper walks into a bar, and says to the bartender, "I hear you have a drink named after me." The bartender smiles. "Yes, we do," he says "You have a drink called a *Melvin*?"

# Toasted Almond (Low Alcohol)

Blend and pour into a large cocktail glass.

| | |
|---|---|
| 2 scoops | French vanilla ice cream |
| 1/3 cup | Ice |
| 2 oz | Cream |
| 1 oz | *Kahlua* |
| 1 oz | Cherry flavored syrup |

Garnish with whipped cream and shaved chocolate or slivered almonds. Drizzle with chocolate syrup and grenadine.

> *Selective memory loss is a great asset when bartending.*
>
> "Hey John, haven't seen you in weeks!" Instead of: "So, you are John's wife? That's funny, you aren't the woman he came in with last night. She was blond, and had really big .....uuummmm, uhhh....."

## Toasted Almond (Non-Alcoholic)

Blend and pour into a large cocktail glass.

| | |
|---|---|
| 2 scoops | French Vanilla ice cream |
| 1/3 cup | Ice |
| 2 oz | Cream |
| 1/2 oz | Coffee flavored syrup |
| 1/2 oz | *Hershey's* chocolate syrup |
| 1 oz | Cherry flavored syrup |

Garnish with whipped cream, drizzle with cherry syrup.

## Toasted Raspberries (Low Alcohol)

Blend and pour into a large cocktail glass.

| | |
|---|---|
| 2 scoops | French Vanilla ice cream |
| 1/3 cup | Ice |
| 2 oz | Cream |
| 3/4 oz | Raspberry flavored syrup |
| 1/4 oz | Coffee flavored syrup |
| 1 oz | Butterscotch Schnapps |

Garnish with whipped cream and raspberry syrup.

## Toasted Raspberries (Non Alcoholic)

In a blender, combine:

| | |
|---|---|
| 2 scoops | French Vanilla ice cream |
| 1/3 cup | Ice |
| 2 oz | Cream |
| 3/4 oz | Raspberry flavored syrup |
| 1 oz | Butterscotch flavored syrup |
| 1/4 oz | Coffee flavored syrup |

Blend and pour into a large cocktail glass. Garnish with whipped cream and drizzle with raspberry syrup.

# Exotic Drinks

## Blue Fish

Hurricane glass, fill with ice. Shake and strain:

2 oz   ***Absolut Citron*** Vodka

1 oz   ***HPNOTIQ***

3 oz   White cranberry juice

Garnish with gummy fish.

## Blue Hawaiian

Tall glass, fill with ice.

1 oz   Rum

1/2 oz   Blue ***Curacao***

2 oz   Sweet and Sour

2 oz   Pineapple juice

Garnish with cherries and orange slices, or slices of pineapple.

## Chi-Chi

In a blender combine:

1 cup   Ice

1 oz   Vodka

1 oz   Crème de Coconut or Chi-Chi mix

2 oz   Pineapple juice

Blend and pour into a large specialty glass. Garnish with cherries and orange slices.

# Fog Cutter

Tall glass, fill with ice.

|         |        |
|---------|--------|
| 1/2 oz  | Brandy |
| 1 oz    | Rum    |
| 1/2 oz  | Gin    |

Fill the glass with equal mix of Sweet and Sour and orange juice. Garnish with cherries and orange slices.

# *HPNOTIQ* Mimosa

Champagne glass, chilled.
Shake with ice and strain:

|       |                      |
|-------|----------------------|
| 1 oz  | *HPNOTIQ*            |
| 2 oz  | Champagne (chilled)  |
| 2 oz  | Orange juice (chilled) |

Garnish with an orange slice.

# Hurricane

Tall glass, fill with ice.

|        |                     |
|--------|---------------------|
| 1 oz   | *Myers'* Rum        |
| 1 oz   | *Bacardi* Light Rum |
| 1/4 oz | Rose's Lime Juice   |

Nearly fill the glass with equal parts of Sweet and Sour and orange juice. Top with 1/2 oz grenadine. Garnish with cherries and orange slices.

# KIR Royal

Champagne glass, chilled, no ice.
Nearly fill the glass with chilled champagne. Top with 1/2 oz *Chambord.* Garnish with cherries.

# Lemon Drop
Rocks glass, fill with ice, sugared rim.

 1 oz    Vodka
 1/2 oz    Triple Sec
 1/2 oz    Lemon juice

Fill the glass with Sweet and Sour. Garnish with lemon slices covered in sugar.

# Mai-Tai
Tall glass, fill with ice

 1 oz    Rum
 1/2 oz    Crème de Noyaux (Almond)
 1/2 oz    Triple Sec

Fill the glass with equal parts of Sweet and Sour and pineapple juice. Top with 1/2 oz *Myers'* Rum. Garnish with cherries.

> Mai-Tais are a fun and exotic drink, known for their brown lid (or top). Floating *Myers'* Rum as the last step creates this distinctive appearance.

# Mimosa
Champagne glass, chilled.
Fill the glass with equal parts of:

 Champagne (chilled)
 Orange juice (chilled)

Garnish with orange slices and cherries.

# Piña Colada

In a blender add:

    1 cup  Ice
    1 oz  Light Rum (or *Malibu*)
    1 oz  Crème de Coconut or Piña Colada mix
    2 oz  Pineapple juice

Blend and pour into a large cocktail glass. Garnish with cherries and orange slices, or pineapple slices.

# Planter's Punch

Tall glass, fill with ice.

    2 dashes  Bitters
    1 oz  *Myers'* Rum

Nearly fill the glass with equal parts orange juice and Sweet and Sour. Top with 1/2 oz grenadine. Garnish with cherries and orange slices.

# Singapore Sling

Tall glass, fill with ice.

    1 oz  Gin
    1/2 oz  Grenadine
    2 oz  Sweet and Sour

Nearly fill the glass with club soda. Top with 1/2 oz cherry or blackberry brandy. Garnish with cherries and orange slices.

# Rum Runner

Tall glass, fill with ice. Layer:

| | |
|---|---|
| 1/2 oz | Light Rum |
| 1/2 oz | Gold Rum |
| 1-1/2 oz | Sweet and Sour |
| 1/2 oz | Blackberry Brandy |
| 1/2 oz | Crème de Banana |

Nearly fill the glass with orange juice. Top with 1/2 oz grenadine. Garnish with cherries and orange slices.

# Rum Runner (Caribbean Style)

Hurricane glass, fill with ice. Layer:

| | |
|---|---|
| 1/2 oz | Pineapple-Coconut Rum |
| 1/2 oz | Strawberry-Kiwi Rum |
| 1/2 oz | Coconut Rum |
| 1/2 oz | Banana Rum |
| 1-1/2 oz | Sweet and Sour |

Nearly fill the glass with orange juice. Top with 1/2 oz grenadine. Garnish with cherries and pineapple slices.

# Rum Runner (San Francisco Style)

Tall glass, fill with ice. Layer:

| | |
|---|---|
| 1/3 oz | Light Rum |
| 1/3 oz | Gold Rum |
| 1/3 oz | 151 Rum |
| 1/3 oz | Coconut Rum |
| 1-1/2 oz | Sweet and Sour |
| 1/4 oz | *Midori* |

Nearly fill the glass with orange juice. Top with 1/2 oz *Chambord* Garnish with cherries and orange slices.

## Sangria

Tall glass, fill with ice.

| | |
|---|---|
| 3-4 oz | Dry red wine |
| 3/4 oz | Peach Schnapps |
| 1-1/2 oz | Orange juice |
| 1-1/2 oz | Sweet and Sour |
| 3/4 oz | Grenadine |
| 3/4 oz | Rose's Lime Juice |

Garnish with orange slices, cherries, lemon and lime wedges.

## Tropical Rum Runner

Hurricane glass, fill with ice. Layer:

| | |
|---|---|
| 1/2 oz | Pineapple-Coconut Rum |
| 1/2 oz | Banana Rum |
| 1/2 oz | Raspberry Rum |
| 1/2 oz | Coconut Rum |
| 1-1/2 oz | Sweet and Sour |

Nearly fill the glass with orange juice. Top with 1/2 oz grenadine. Garnish with cherries and orange slices.

## Very Berry Rum Runner

Hurricane glass, fill with ice. Layer:

| | |
|---|---|
| 1/2 oz | Strawberry-Kiwi Rum |
| 1/2 oz | Strawberry-Banana Rum |
| 1/2 oz | Coconut Rum |
| 1-1/2 oz | Sweet and Sour |

Nearly fill the glass with orange juice. Top with 1/2 oz raspberry syrup Garnish with cherries and orange slices.

## Zipper

Tall glass, fill with ice. Layer:

| | |
|---|---|
| 1/3 oz | Vanilla Rum |
| 1/3 oz | Coconut Rum |
| 1/3 oz | Light Rum |
| 1/4 oz | Raspberry Vodka |
| 1-1/2 oz | Sweet and Sour |
| 1/4 oz | *99 Bananas* |

Nearly fill the glass with orange juice. Top with 1/2 oz *Chambord* Garnish with cherries and orange slices.

## Zombie

Tall glass, fill with ice.

| | |
|---|---|
| 1 oz | Rum |
| 1/2 oz | Crème de Noyaux (Almond) |
| 1/2 oz | Triple Sec |

Nearly fill the glass with even mix of orange juice and Sweet and Sour. Top with 1/2 oz *Bacardi* 151 rum. Garnish with cherries.

---

### A Quick Table for Some Popular Shooters

*Kahlua + Bailey's +*

| | | |
|---|---|---|
| Vodka | = | Mudslide |
| *Grand Marnier* | = | B-52 |
| *Crown Royal* | = | Duck Fart |
| Crème de Banana | = | Monkey Fart |
| *99 Bananas* | = | Gorilla Fart |
| *Frangelico* | = | German Chocolate Cake |
| Butterscotch Schnapps | = | Goldrush |
| *Baja Rosa* | = | Neapolitan |

# Shooters

There are several ways to make beautifully layers shooters. The most important thing is to slow the rate that the liqueur pours into the shot glass, to keep the layers from mixing. It is hard to free pour while doing this, so use your eye and make a "best guess" as to when you have added enough.

## 1. <u>Cherries</u>

Pour the bottom layer of liqueur into a shot glass. Suspend the cherry over the shot glass, holding it by the stem. Slowly pour the next layer of liqueur over the cherry, slowing the rate the liqueur pours into the glass. Pour the next layer in the same fashion.

If you are going to give the cherry to your customer, set it in a separate shot glass. If you set it in the layered shooter you just made, the weight of the cherry will mess up the look of the drink.

It is not acceptable to eat the cherry yourself, while you are working.

## 2. <u>Spoons</u>

Pour the bottom layer of liqueur into a shot glass. While holding a spoon by the handle, slowly pour the next layer over the <u>back</u> of the spoon. Pour the next layer in the same fashion. Resist the temptation to lick the spoon.

## 3. <u>Using the side of the glass</u>

Pour the bottom layer of liqueur into a shot glass. While tipping the glass about 30 degrees, slowly pour the next layer. The liqueur should slide down the side of the glass and float on the previous layer. This method leaves a "trail" down the side of the glass, spoiling the layered look on one side, but, is good to know if you are in a hurry and don't have a spoon or cherry handy.

For best results, pour the heaviest layers first, such as **Kahlua** and **Bailey's** Irish Cream. Of the two, **Kahlua** should always be poured first.

## Apple Pie

Shot glass, no ice. Layer:

    1/3 oz    **Bailey's** Irish Cream  (bottom)
    1/3 oz    Apple Schnapps  (middle)
    1/3 oz    **Goldschlager**  (top)

Top with whipped cream.

## Apple-Peach Pie

Shot glass, no ice. Layer:

    1/3 oz    **Bailey's** Irish Cream (bottom)
    1/3 oz    Apple Schnapps  (next)
    1/3 oz    Peach Schnapps  (next)
    1/8 oz    **Goldschlager**  (top)

Top with whipped cream.

## B-52

Shot glass, no ice. Layer:

    1/3 oz    **Kahlua**  (bottom)
    1/3 oz    **Bailey's** Irish Cream  (middle)
    1/3 oz    **Grand Marnier**  (top)

# Blow Job

Shot glass, no ice. Layer:

1/3 oz   *Bailey's* Irish Cream (bottom)
1/3 oz   Amaretto (middle)
1/3 oz   *Frangelico* (top)

Top with 4-6" of whipped cream

# Brain Hemorrhage *Creepy!*

Shot glass, no ice.

3/4 oz   Peach Schnapps

Float 1/4 oz grenadine on top of the schnapps, than pour several large dollops of Irish Cream into the glass. You want the Irish Cream to break through the grenadine and mix with the schnapps. The Irish Cream will immediately form weird little white globs with trails of red.

# Bubblegum

Shot glass, no ice. Layer:

1/3 oz   *Bailey's* Irish Cream (bottom)
1/3 oz   Blue *Curacao* (middle)
1/3 oz   Crème de Banana (top)

# Buttery Nipple (Butter Babies)

Shot glass, no ice. Layer:

1/3 oz   *Bailey's* Irish Cream (bottom)
2/3 oz   Butterscotch Schnapps (top)

## Caramel Apple Pie
Shot glass, no ice. Layer:

1/4 oz   ***Bailey's*** Irish Cream   (bottom)
1/4 oz   Apple Schnapps   (next)
1/4 oz   Butterscotch Schnapps   (next)
1/4 oz   ***Goldschlager***   (top)

Top with whipped cream.

## Cement Mixer
Shot glass.

1 oz   ***Bailey's*** Irish Cream
1/4 oz   Rose's Lime Juice

Allow this drink a minute or so to set up. The lime juice will curdle the cream into a tasty, but rather solid lump. An old time party joke.

## Chocolate Cake
Shot glass, no ice. Sugared rim.

2/3 oz   ***Absolut Citron*** Vodka
1/3 oz   ***Frangelico***

Serve with several sugared lemon slices.

## Cowboy Cocksucker
Shot glass, no ice. Layer:

1/3 oz   ***Bailey's*** Irish Cream   (bottom)
1/3 oz   Vodka   (middle)
1/3 oz   Butterscotch Schnapps   (top)

Top with 4-6" of whipped cream

# Dr. Pepper
Shot glass, no ice. Layer:

1/2 oz   ***Bailey's*** Irish Cream   (bottom)
1/4 oz   Amaretto   (middle)
1/4 oz   ***Yukon Jack*** Whiskey   (top)

# Duck Farts
Shot glass, no ice. Layer:

1/3 oz   ***Kahlua***   (bottom)
1/3 oz   ***Bailey's*** Irish Cream   (middle)
1/3 oz   ***Crown Royal*** Whiskey   (top)

# German Chocolate Cake
Shot glass, no ice. Layer:

1/3 oz   ***Kahlua***   (bottom)
1/3 oz   ***Bailey's*** Irish Cream   (middle)
1/3 oz   ***Frangelico***   (top)

Top with whipped cream.

# Goldrush
Shot glass, no ice. Layer:

1/3 oz   ***Kahlua***   (bottom)
1/3 oz   ***Bailey's*** Irish Cream   (middle)
1/3 oz   Butterscotch Schnapps   (top)

# Harley Davidson

Shot glass, no ice. Layer:

| | |
|---|---|
| 1/2 oz | *Jack Daniel's* Whiskey |
| 1/2 oz | *Yukon Jack* Whiskey |

# Kamikaze

Shot glass, no ice. Layer:

| | |
|---|---|
| 1 oz | Vodka |
| 1/2 oz | Triple Sec |
| 1/4 oz | Rose's Lime Juice |

Garnish with a lime wedge.

# Jell-O Shooters

| | |
|---|---|
| 1 box | Jell-O (any flavor) |
| 2/3 cup | Vodka (or other hard liquor) |
| 1 cup | Hot water |

Make the Jell-O according the instructions on the box. Replace the cold water with the liquor. Pour the mix into small Dixie cups or other small plastic cups. Chill according to the Jell-O directions.

For best results, keep all of one kind of liquor the same flavors. For example, tequila with lime Jell-O, vodka with grape, etc. One really good combination is apricot Jell-O with peach schnapps.

## Jell-O Shooters 2 (Party Mix)

| 3 boxes | Jell-O |
|---|---|
| 2 cups | Vodka (or other hard liquor) |
| 3 cups | Hot water |

Boil the water and add the Jell-O, stirring constantly. After the Jell-O has dissolved, stir for another 2 minutes, then add the vodka. Stir well, about a minute, then pour into small Dixie cups, or small plastic condiment containers.

> The alcohol in the shooters is not burned off. Consider 4 Jell-O shooters as equal to drinking a full shot of 86 proof liquor.

## Key Lime Pie

Shot glass, no ice. Serve with lime slices.

| 3/4 oz | *Smirnoff Lime Twist* Vodka |
|---|---|
| 1/4 oz | *Stoli* Vanilla Vodka |
| 1/4 oz | Butterscotch Schnapps |

## Lemon Meringue Pie

Shot glass, no ice. Serve with lemon slices.

| 3/4 oz | *Absolut Citron* Vodka |
|---|---|
| 1/4 oz | *Stoli* Vanilla Vodka |
| 1/4 oz | Butterscotch Schnapps |

## Liquid Cocaine

Shot glass, no ice. Layer:

| 1/3 oz | *Jagermeister* (bottom) |
|---|---|
| 1/3 oz | *Rumplemintz* (middle) |
| 1/3 oz | *Bacardi* 151 Rum (top) |

## Lovers' Hearts

Shot glass, no ice.

> 3/4 oz    Peach Schnapps

Float 1/4 oz grenadine, than add several large dollops of **Baja Rosa** Strawberry Cream Tequila, or **Baja Luna** Raspberry Cream Tequila. When the tequila breaks through the grenadine and mixes with the schnapps, it will immediately form little pink or purple blobs.

## Mexican Hooters

Shot glass, no ice.

> 1 oz    Tequila
> 2 Tbs    Cottage Cheese

Top with red or green Tabasco Sauce.

## Mind Eraser

Rocks glass, fill with ice. Layer:

> 1/2 oz    **Kahlua** (bottom)
> 1/3 oz    Vodka (middle)

Top with club soda.

## Monkey Farts

Shot glass, no ice. Layer:

> 1/3 oz    **Kahlua** (bottom)
> 1/3 oz    **Bailey's** Irish Cream (middle)
> 1/3 oz    Crème de Banana (top)

## Mud Slide

Shot glass, no ice. Layer:

1/3 oz   ***Kahlua*** (bottom)
1/3 oz   ***Bailey's*** Irish Cream  (middle)
1/3 oz   Vodka (top)

## Muff Diver

Shot glass, no ice. Layer:

1/3 oz   ***Bailey's*** Irish Cream  (bottom)
1/3 oz   Amaretto (middle)
1/3 oz   Butterscotch Schnapps (top)

Top with 4-6" of whipped cream

## 911

Shot glass, no ice. Layer:

1/3 oz   ***Jagermeister*** (bottom)
1/3 oz   ***Goldschlager*** (middle)
1/3 oz   ***Rumplemintz*** (top)

## Oatmeal Cookie

Shot glass, no ice. Layer:

1/4 oz   ***Kahlua*** (bottom)
1/4 oz   ***Bailey's*** Irish Cream (next)
1/4 oz   Butterscotch Schnapps (next)
1/4 oz   ***Goldschlager*** (top)

## Oatmeal Cookie 2

Shot glass, no ice. Layer:

1/4 oz   *Jagermeister* (bottom)
1/4 oz   *Bailey's* Irish Cream  (next)
1/4 oz   Butterscotch Schnapps  (next)
1/4 oz   *Goldschlager*  (top)

## Pineapple Upside Down Cake

Shot glass, chilled, no ice. Shake with ice and strain:

1/2 oz   Pineapple juice
1/2 oz   *Stoli* Vanilla Vodka
1 splash   Grenadine

## Prairie Fire

Shot glass, no ice.

1 oz   Tequila

Top with red or green Tabasco Sauce.

## Prison Sex

Shot glass, no ice. Layer:

3/4 oz   Butterscotch Schnapps  (bottom)
1/4 oz   *Crown Royal* Whiskey  (top)

## Red Headed Slut

Shot glass, no ice. Shake with ice and strain:

1/4 oz   *Jagermeister*
3/4 oz   Peach Schnapps
1/4 oz   Cranberry Juice

# Screaming Orgasm

Shot glass, no ice. Layer:

| | |
|---|---|
| 1/4 oz | **Kahlua** (bottom) |
| 1/4 oz | **Bailey's** Irish Cream (next) |
| 1/4 oz | Amaretto (next) |
| 1/4 oz | Vodka (top) |

# Silk Panties

Shot glass, no ice.

| | |
|---|---|
| 1/2 oz | Peach Schnapps |
| 1/2 oz | Vodka |

# Slippery Nipple

Shot glass, no ice. Layer:

| | |
|---|---|
| 1/3 oz | **Bailey's** Irish Cream (bottom) |
| 2/3 oz | **Sambuca** (top) |

# Surfer on Acid

Shot glass, no ice. Layer:

| | |
|---|---|
| 1/3 oz | **Jagermeister** (bottom) |
| 1/3 oz | **Malibu** Rum (middle) |
| 1/3 oz | Pineapple juice (top) |

# Scooby Snacks

Shot glass, no ice. Layer:

| | |
|---|---|
| 1/3 oz | **Malibu** Rum (bottom) |
| 1/3 oz | **Midori** (middle) |
| 1/3 oz | Cream (top) |

# Tootsie Roll

Rocks glass, no ice.

>   1 oz    *Kahlua*

Fill the glass with orange juice.

# Washington Apple

Shot glass, no ice.

>   1/3 oz    *Southern Comfort*
>   1/3 oz    *Sour Apple Puckers*
>   1/3 oz    Cranberry juice

# Washington Apple 2

Shot glass, no ice.

>   1/3 oz    *Crown Royal* Whiskey
>   1/3 oz    *Sour Apple Puckers*
>   1/3 oz    Cranberry juice

# A Brief Introduction to Liquors, Wines and Beers

During my research, I found a number of fun and interesting sources of facts, figures and folklore. This section is a brief compilation of the wide variety, and often conflicting, information I found.

## Beer

The main ingredients in beer are malted barley, hops, yeast, water, and corn. Each of these items can significantly alter the taste of the end product. For example, the type of water used in the brewing process, is it distilled, or natural spring water? Is it from the Rocky Mountains or imported from France?

The type, age, quality of the grains, even the growing conditions for any particular year can affect the taste, as can the quantities used for each particular recipe.

Other ingredients may be added to make the brew unique, such as fruits, berries and vegetables. Apricot, strawberry, peach, mango, cherry, blueberry, cranberry, orange, orange cream, blackberry, plum, banana, apple, raspberry, grape, boysenberry, and even watermelon beers can be found at specialty breweries.

Small, specialty breweries are called microbreweries, or craft breweries.

Many people brew beer at home as a weekend hobby. Unlike hard liquor, which has strict production control, beer can legally be produced in a person's home for private consumption. **These home brews are not for sale to the public.**

Fruit beers are especially popular with home brewing enthusiasts, and sometimes the response to a new flavor is so great that it inspires a new microbrewery. To date, there are hundreds, if not thousands, of microbreweries across the United States.

Spice, herb and vegetable beers can also be found in many microbreweries. Some of the most popular beers include pumpkin, chocolate, coconut, garlic, sage, coriander, vanilla, and honey.

Light beers, with their lower calorie, lower carbohydrate properties, have gained in popularity as more people are become increasingly health conscience. Many people, however, assume they can drink more quantity, since it is a "light" beer, which tends to compromise the benefits. It should be noted that "light" beer does not necessarily mean less alcohol.

- **Ale** - A flavorful and lightly scented beer with a slightly stronger hops flavor then most domestic beers. The alcohol content is generally 4 – 5%.

  This beer is best served with hearty meat dishes such as beef, turkey, chicken, lamb, pork and salmon.

- **DPA** (Draft Pale Ale) - A dark, Irish styled beer, with an alcohol content about 5.1%.

  The best foods to serve with this beer include steaks, spicy BBQ, and Italian dishes such as pizza.

- **English Ale** - The traditional beer of Great Britain. English Ales tend to be dark brown in color, and slightly sweet in flavor. The alcohol content is between 4 - 5%.

  This beer is best served with meat and bread dishes such as Yorkshire Pudding, roast beef and potatoes, hamburgers, turkey with stuffing, breaded chicken, lamb pie, and stuffed salmon.

- **Fruit Ale** – An ale which has been combined with a variety of fruits such as apricots and peaches. As a result, fruit ales are slightly sweeter then traditional ales.

  The best foods to serve with this beer are light appetizers, salads, and desserts, such as pies and pastries.

- **IPA** **(India Pale Ale)** – An aromatic ale, with a very hoppy flavor. The IPA alcohol content is about 6.7%.

  India Pale Ale originated in Great Britain during the 1800's, in response to the demands of their military. Apparently, the troops threatened to leave India unless they received some good beer.

  IPAs were developed using Tomahawk hops. These stronger hops helped to keep the brew stabilized during the long voyage.

  The best foods to serve with this beer are meaty dishes, such as BBQ ribs, lasagna, beef, pheasant, duck, turkey, chicken, lamb, pork and salmon.

- **Domestics** – These beers are brewed in the United States. They are usually pasteurized, have a lower alcohol level then a lager or ale, and are commonly a pale gold in color.

  These light beers go well with a wide variety of foods. Some of the best combinations include pizza, sub sandwiches, hamburgers, steak, turkey, duck, chicken, pork, shellfish, salmon, spicy Asian and Mexican dishes, and anything cooked on the BBQ.

- **Hefeweizen** **(Weizen)** – The traditional beer of Bavaria. This beer is unfiltered making it slightly thicker with more body than a regular beer. It has a cloudy appearance, is quite effervescent, has a pleasing fruity taste, and a thick, foamy head. The alcohol content is about 5.2%.

  Hefeweizen is traditionally served with lemon slices.

  The best foods to serve with this beer are beef, pork, salmon, grilled tuna, swordfish, shark, salads, chicken, turkey, game hens, and spicy German, Finnish or Russian dishes.

- **Pilsner or Lager** – These beers are allowed to ferment a second time, usually for several months. The result is a smoother, more full-bodied flavor. They have a medium to light hops flavor, and the coloring ranges from light blond to pale gold. Their alcohol content is about 5%.

  The best foods to serve with this beer are appetizers, cheese, crab, lobster, mussels, shrimp, oysters, and hot, spicy dishes.

- **Porter** – A heavy bodied, very dark beer, tasting strongly of malt. The alcohol content is about 5%.

  The best foods to serve with this beer are BBQ ribs, steak, pork, chicken, turkey, and spicy Mexican entrees.

  Most foods need to be strongly flavored to avoid being overpowered by this beer, with the exception of traditional Norwegian lutefisk and lefse, which seem to become more palatable the stronger the beer is.

- **SHV** – Spice, Herb & Vegetable beers.

- **Storage** – Many beers are unpasturized and need to be kept cold, in a dark environment for best flavor. This is why most commercially bottled beers come in dark bottles and are kept in the refrigerated section of your grocery.

  Beer is perishable, and should be consumed as soon as possible after purchase. For best flavor, beer should be stored at temperatures between 48 to 55 degrees.

- **Stout** – A very dark beer (nearly black) with a very strong flavor of hops, and may taste somewhat bitter. The alcohol content is quite high, between 5 - 6 1/2%.

  The best foods to serve with this beer are BBQ ribs, steak, pork, chicken, turkey, and spicy Asian, Italian or Mexican entrees. The food will need to be strongly flavored to avoid being overpowered by this beer.

- **Taste** - The flavor of the beer. The most common flavors or scents come from the strength levels of the malt and hops. While malt has a sweet scent, similar to fresh baked bread, hops produce a citrus type scent, similar to grapefruit and lemons.

## Proper Beer Service

- **Bottled Beer** - When serving beer in a bottle, always remove the cap for the customer. Serve frosty cold, and provide a chilled glass, if requested.

  Check the bottle top for any chips or places where the glass lip may have broken during transportation or uncapping. If a chip is found, discard the bottle and get a new one. Never serve any drink from a chipped or broken bottle. This does <u>not</u> mean simply pouring the beer into a glass. You cannot see the broken glass if it is in the beer. Throw it away.

- **Corona** - Serve in the bottle, with a lime wedge.

- **Canned Beer** - Always open the can for the customer, and serve with a chilled glass, if requested. Do not shake the can before opening.

- **Guinness** - Serve in the can, with a chilled glass.

- **Hefeweizen** - Serve with several lemon wedges.

- **Tap Beer** - Always serve draft beer in a clean, chilled glass. The foam head should be approximately 1/2"high. Be sure to serve with a coaster as draft beers tend to sweat. Give the customer and clean, chilled glass with each refill.

# The Story of the
# Adolph Coors' Brewing Company

In 1873, Adolph Coors, only 26 years old, founded the Coors' Brewing Company, in Golden Colorado. Grown to become the largest single site brewery in the world, Coors' was originally marketing to the miners working in the Rocky Mountains. Delivered by mules, trains and wagons, the brewery quickly made a name for itself. Soon, settlers in the Western states also became familiar with the Coors' name and quality beverages.

During Prohibition, the brewery continued to grow by producing other food products such as malted milk and a near beer, called Mannah. Coors' was one of very few breweries to survive the long 18 years of Prohibition.

In 1959, Coors' started the first recycling program in the country. Offering 1 cent for each can returned.

Adolph's grandson Bill, played a major role in the development of the Coors' Company. In 1959, Coors' produced the first 2-part aluminum can. Bill was instrumental in designing the aluminum can, a revolutionary concept, which allowed Coors' to produce packaged, draft quality beers for large scale markets. The design of this aluminum can is still a standard in the beer industry today.

Bill, always concerned about his employees and their families, introduced one of the first on-site corporate wellness centers in the United States.

Until the 1970's, Coors' was available only in the Western United States. People on the East Coast had to find their own way to get the beer home. One fan was President Ford, who was rumored to regularly ship back several cases aboard Air Force One, when returning from visits in Colorado.

Gradually, Coors' increased production and expanded their distribution network. Kicking off this expansion was a new marketing campaign showcasing a lower calorie beer, packaged in a bright, silver can. Coors' Light was an immediate success. Sales skyrocketed with the introduction of "the Silver Bullet"

Today, Coors' is still known for producing their beers at a chilly 32 degrees, using pure, natural Rocky Mountain spring water. Coors' is ranked third in national beer sales, and is listed on the New York Stock Exchange under the symbol **RKY**.

## Sources

"Coors Brewing Company: Celebrating 125 Years of Brewing Excellence," *Rocky Mountain Beer Notes*, April 1998, <http://www.beernotes.com/rockymtn/ articles/ 000324.html>, (04 April 2004).

"Coors Organization/History," *Birmingham Beverage Company*, <http://www.alabev.com/coorsorg.htm>, (04 April 2004).

---

# The Story of the
# Anheuser-Busch Brewing Company

---

In 1860, Eberhard Anheuser bought the barely functioning St. Louis Brewery. Four years later, Adolphus Busch, only 20 years old, joined him.

Right away there was a problem. The beer they were making was not very good. Together, they began searching for a better recipe. This trek led them to the city of Budweis, in the Czech Republic. Finding a wonderful brew, they obtained the recipe, and started making the beer that would later be named Budweiser.

The teamwork of Eberhard and Adolphus proved quite successful, and as the beer improved, the fledgling company grew.

But there was more then beer on the mind of young Adolphus, namely, Eberhard's very pretty daughter, Lily. It came as no surprise when Adolphus asked for her hand, and within months, the two were married.

In 1876, the name Budweiser was trademarked by Anheuser-Busch.

During this growth period, the company bought quite a bit of real estate. During Prohibition, the brewery survived by producing non-alcoholic beers and selling property which had previous housed saloons.

In 1933, the famous Budweiser Clydesdales were introduced. These beautiful horses have been credited with re-establishing the popularity of the draft horse in America today.

Standing 6 feet tall at the shoulder and weighing between 2,000 and 2,300 pounds, the Budweiser Clydesdales are an impressive display of sheer horsepower.

More then 35 Clydesdale mares, stallions and foals are kept at the famous Budweiser Clydesdale Stables. Owning nearly 250 of the famous horses, Anheuser-Busch has one of the largest herds of Clydesdale horses in the world.

Before trucks were invented to deliver the beer, delivery wagons were used. A Dalmatian dog always rode with the team. His duty was to protect the valuable horses and cargo from theft, while the driver was making his deliveries. If you look closely, you will see a Dalmatian riding in the wagon or sleigh, anytime the Budweiser Clydesdales are performing.

Paving the way to destiny? According to rumor, immediately after August III was born, and before he was allowed to nurse for the first time, his father gave him an eyedropper of Budweiser beer. I guess you would call that beer with a milk chaser.

In 1953, August Busch, Jr. purchased the St. Louis Cardinals baseball team. Busch was very fond of the team and attended many of their games. He was known for arriving in a wagon pulled by the spirited Budweiser Clydesdales.

Many baseball legends have played with the St. Louis Cardinals, including Cy Young who played with the team from 1899-1901.

A long time baseball fan, August closely followed the Brooklyn Dodgers and their star player Jackie Robinson. Upon asking the team's management how many blacks were playing for them, he was outraged to find out that there were none. He made his feeling known and as a result, in 1954, the Cardinals welcomed their first black player.

August was loved my fans and team members alike. To this day, during the seventh inning stretch at Busch Stadium, instead of playing "Take Me out to the Ball Game," they play the trademark Budweiser theme song, "Here Comes the King."

In 1969, Anheuser-Busch entered Miss Budweiser in her first hydroplane race.

An icon of Americana, Miss Budweiser has been seen in thousands of parades around the country and is often on display, when not actually racing.

In 1989, the "King of Beers" promotion was started. This promotion skyrocketed Budweiser to become the nation's largest brewery.

In March 2004, the Miss Budweiser team broke the world speed record for Unlimited hydroplane racing. The previous record had stood for 42 years.

Considered by many to be the most successful Unlimited hydroplane racing team in history, in 41 seasons, Miss Budweiser entered 360 races, winning 136 times and finishing in the top three 234 times. In addition, the team has also won 23 World Championships, and carried away the prestigious APBA Gold Cup 14 times.

Today, Budweiser holds at least 45% of the domestic beer market, and one out of every two beers sold in the United States is said to be an Anheuser-Busch product.

Anheuser-Busch employs over 23,000 people nationwide, and is listed as one of the largest companies in the United States. Budweiser is publicly traded on the New York Stock Exchange under the symbol **BUD**.

## Sources

"Clydesdale Stables, Grant's Farm," *Anheuser-Busch Inc.*, <http://www.grantsfarm.com/docs/stables.htm>, (1 May 2004).

"Famous Budweiser Clydesdales," *Budweiser Company, a division of Anheuser-Busch Inc.*, <http://www.budweisertours.com/ docs/clydes.htm>, (2 May 2004).

"Hydroplane racing - Miss Budweiser shatters world speed record for kilometer run," *Detroit News Motor Sports*, 14 March 2004, <http://www.detnews.com/ 2004/motorsports/0403/17/motorsports-91404.htm>, (14 April 2004).

Jonah Goldberg, "Buds for life, A man and his beer," *National Review - Online*, 25 September 2000, <http://www.national review.com/25sept00/goldberg092500.shtml>, (3 May 2004).

"King of Beers – History Timeline," *Budweiser Company, a division of Anheuser-Busch Inc.*, <http://www.budweiser.ca/ kob_history.html>, (25 April 2004).

"The APBA Gold Cup. History - Powerboat Racing," *Hickok Sports*, <http://www.hickoksports.com/ history/pbgoldcup.shtml>, (25 April 2004).

"Today in History March 28, A Baseball Brew,*" Library of Congress American Memory Collections,* <http://memory .loc.gov/ammem/today/mar28.html>, (21 April 2004).

# Brandy and Cognac

Brandy is a sophisticated liquor made from grape wine. The wine base is usually made from grapes that are white, as they tend to produce a more flavorful product, with less bitterness, then red grapes. Brandies are often distilled with concentrated fruit extracts such as apples, berries, cherries, peaches and apricots

Brandies tend to be regional in production, based on the available fruits in the area. If the bottle label reads "Brandy," then the product must be made solely from grapes. If other fruits are added the type or types must be included in the name, for example, *"Peach Brandy"* or *"Apricot Brandy."*

Brandy is aged in oak barrels for 3-8 years. Caramel may be added to give the brandy a characteristic soft brown color.

Cognac is a brandy distilled in Cognac, France. Cognac is given a rating based on the quality – a "3 Star" is lowest, followed by VSOP (Very Superior Old Pale). Champagne, a cognac distilled in the Champagne region of France, is considered the highest grade.

# Gin

Gin is a hard liquor made from a variety of grains. The distillate vapor is passed through a combination of Juniper berries and herbs, giving it a very distinctive flavor.

# A Little History of Gin

The actual birthplace of gin is unknown (many countries claim that honor). It is most widely accepted to have started in China or Arabia in the 13th Century.

During the 1600's a ban was placed on the importation of French brandy into England, and heavy taxes were placed on German liquors. This ensured that Dutch gin had a very strong market. Who says there is no such connection between sex, alcohol and money? The primary push for these bans and taxes were from the DUTCH consort to the English queen. Shortly following these changes, the taxes on BRITISH beers were raised, effectively making DUTCH gin, called "Dutch Courage," the cheapest and most widely consumed beverage in all of Great Britain. Does anyone else see a slight "conflict of interest" here?

In the 1700's Britain began having serious problems with the abuse of this potent liquor. As the working class became more and more dissatisfied, the drunkenness became epidemic. To put this in perspective: in the late 1600's the consumption of gin, in London alone, was about 500,000 gallons. By the 1750's this amount had climbed to over 11 million gallons.

In 1820, James Burroughs, a pharmacist, developed what was to become one of the leading English gins. He built his distillery near the Thames River and the Tower of London. He had developed the recipe for his gin, but did not yet have a trademark name for his fine liquor. One day, deep in thought, he took a walk along the road to the Queen's palace. While watching the changing of the guards, he noted the exceptionally strong and fierce Yeomen (soldiers) guarding the Royal Palace, and inquired about them. A local merchant told him that the Yeomen were so tough because they ate a full ration of beef every day, so much meat that they were called "beef eaters." Today, the symbol of the Yeoman graces each and every Beefeater Gin bottle.

In 1860, a bartender in San Francisco, California created the first martini.

Around 1825, tonic water was invented. Tonic water was first called Indian Tonic Water, and was made with Quinine to help prevent Malaria in the East Indian jungles.

The taste of Quinine is quite bitter. To get the soldiers to drink the tonic water, it was mixed with gin. This quickly became a popular combination.

Another problem was to get the men to eat citrus fruits to help fight scurvy, an illness common on long ship voyages, caused by a lack of vitamin C. Again, gin came to the rescue. Thus was born the *"gin and tonic with a twist of lime."*

How popular was this new combination? Well, as Winston Churchill once said, "The gin and tonic has saved more Englishmen's lives, and minds, than all the doctors in the empire."

Gin is fairly easily distilled. During Prohibition, people often made it in their homes, hence the name "Bathtub Gin."

## Sources

"Beefeater Gin," *Thomas Lowndes & Co. Ltd.* (a subsidiary of Allied Domecq Spirits & Wine Ltd.), <http://www.thomas lowndes.com/beefeater.html>, (4 April 2004).

Cecil Adams, "Will the quinine in tonic water prevent malaria?," *The Straight Dope, a division of Chicago Reader, Inc.*, 13 August 1999, <http://www.straight dope.com/classics/a990813.html>, (21 April 2004).

Craig Melhoff, "Cure for what ails you? Why gin and tonic isn't covered by your medical benefits," *The National Pist*, <http://www.pist. ca/news/gin.html>, (3 April 2004).

"Gin and Tonic," *Science Daily LLC*, <http://www.sciencedaily. com/encyclopedia/ gin_and_tonic>, (2 April 2004).

Grant Deegan, "From the Bathtub to the Boardroom: Gin and its History," *Pimp Works*, <http://www.pimpworks.org/~vincent /historymain. html#gin>, (15 April 2004).

"James Burrough – the Founder," *Beefeater Gin*, <http://beefeatergin. com>, (15 March 2004).

"Tonic Water," *Science Daily LLC*, <http://www.science daily.com/ encyclopedia/tonic_water>, (2 April 2004).

# Rum

Rum is a liquor produced from sugar cane, or a combination of molasses and sugar cane. Drinks using rum tend to be quite exotic, as many of the recipes come from the ports of call in the Caribbean, Virgin Islands, and Puerto Rico. Light rums are typically aged one to two years and gold rums three years.

# A Little History of Rum

The rum trade in the early 1700's was the basis for much of the ocean trade between the Caribbean Islands, Europe and the early settlers in the United States. Rum was very profitable, and readily traded for spices and silks, which were highly valued in Europe and the Americas.

The European – Caribbean – New Orleans trading triangle was filled with a variety of players. The huge, Spanish galleons of the merchant shipping companies, renegade privateers with fast, light ships called Rum Runners, the military – trying to extract taxes (and maintain some kind of law and order), and pirates trying to steal the ships and wares. Many stories of high seas adventures, battles, and sunken treasures came from this era.

To avoid taxation, (and jail time for running illegal liquor), many captains never registered their ships. As a result, it is unknown how many ships went down in battles or storms. Speculation has the number ranging in the thousands. The wreckage of these ships litter the ocean floor, particularly off the coasts of Florida. Every once in a while a storm or shifting of the island sands will reveal the remnants of a once proud ship.

It is interesting to note that the main trade routes took the ships back and forth through the Bermuda Triangle, which might explain the phantom ships that were frequently reported.

There is always speculation on the treasures that went down with the ships. Fortunes in gold, silver and gems, lost forever in the dark, cold depths of the unforgiving sea. Pirates' plunder. Unimaginable treasures, never to be seen again.

Many ships of that time had incredibly intricate figureheads – carved from hardwood – adorning their prow (front of the ship). Figureheads were common on Viking ships, usually in the form of a dragon or other similar creature. The purpose was to frighten away evil spirits that might harm the crew. This tradition was passed down for centuries.

European ships tended to have figureheads of beautiful women, often with wings, like an angel. Rather then to scare away evil spirits, their purpose was to provide Divine protection for the ship and crew. Their distinctive figureheads have identified many shipwrecks.

Few ships could be identified by specific registry, as the captain's often changed alliances as quickly as they changed their flags. Pirates often flew flags of friendly countries to lure other ships to come in close enough to be taken. Suddenly the guns were aimed at the unsuspecting ship and the "skull and crossbones" (the flag of the pirate) was raised. The large galleons (big freighting ships) were no match for the faster pirate vessels. The battles were fierce. Sometimes, both ships and crews were lost. If the pirate ship was victorious, those from the merchant ship that survived the battle were made "to walk the plank." This was no laughing matter. The plank was a long board extending off the back of the ship. Falling from that height often proved fatal, not to mention the sharks circling in wait. Very few men survived. From their stories came the legends of the crew's valiant fight and the violence of the pirates.

Many books have been written, and movies made, about the heroes, pirates, treasures, and romantic tropical islands. Stories of "Blackbeard the Pirate" (his real name was Edward Teach) and Captain Bly came from this time. One famous icon still used today is Captain Morgan, the dashing pirate, with his stash of Puerto Rican spiced rum.

## The Story of the
# Bacardi Rums

The Bacardi recipes follow a wild and tense history. The original formulation was created in 1862, by Don Facundo Bacardi Massó, while in Spain. Don Massó later immigrated to Cuba.

While in Cuba, several family members were imprisoned during the Spanish-Cuban wars, and were not freed until the Cuban independence in 1898. It is not known if the imprisonments were the result of the family members personal political opinions, or an attempt by the government to force Don Massó to reveal the incredibly valuable recipes.

Because of the extreme political turmoil, it was not safe to have the recipes where anyone could find them. For nearly a hundred years, it was rumored that the original recipes were never written down, but were passed for generations from father to son in deathbed confessions.

Working late nights at the distillery was lonely for Don Bacardi. At some point, he befriended a family of fruit bats who were living in the dusty distillery rafters. Apparently this friendship blossomed to become quite an ongoing relationship. Don Bacardi later designed the famous Bacardi logo, a large black bat, in remembrance of his furry friends.

In 1950, Henri Schueg married into the family, and took over the business. Henri built the famous Bacardi Distillery in Havana, and began making other products – including beer. In 1960, with the takeover of Cuba by Castro, the distillery was moved to the Bahamas, later diversifying to distilleries in Mexico, Brazil, Puerto Rico, and Miami.

## Sources

Brian Smith, "The History of Bacardi Rum," *PageWise, Inc*, 2002, <http://md.essortment.com/historybacardi_ rwng.htm>, (6 March 2004).

GNS, "Rum lords: History of Bacardi Terror," *Hindustan Times Ltd*, 13 April, <http://www.hindust antimes.com/news/5922_680 719,0015002100000 121.htm>, (30 April 2004).

"Today, the Bacardi Bat is a welcomed character in over 170 countries worldwide," *Bacardi Worldwide*, <http://www.bacardi.ca /batorigins.asp?cityID=1& ticket=>, (5 April 2004).

# Tequila

Tequila is a tasty liquor produced from the sap of the Blue Agave (a desert plant, which grows wildly in the Southwestern United States and Mexico). Contrary to popular belief, Blue Agave is not a member of the cactus family it is actually related to the lily and amaryllis. The Blue Agave is also known as the American Aloe.

To be called "tequila" the liquor must be distilled near the city of Tequila, Mexico. Tequilas made in other parts of Mexico are called Mescal (or Mezcal). Tequila is generally unaged, producing a clear liquor. Tequilas become golden when aged in used whiskey barrels.

## A Little History of Tequila

The history of tequila is a tumultuous as the history of Mexico. Tequila was originally a drink primarily favored by the locals and bandidos (bandits) that inhabited the Mexican countryside.

In 1758, a young man by the name of Jose Antonio Cuervo received permission from the King of Spain to start producing tequila as a product for exporting. Jose became the first licensed manufacturer of tequila, and to this day, his company is still the largest producer of tequila in the world.

The United States became one of the largest buyers of tequila, both because of the building Mexican population, and also because Americans began to develop a taste for this unique liquor.

Tequila's popularity in the United States steadily grew during the late 1800's and early 1900's. During Prohibition, tequila and mescal became even more popular, leading to rampant smuggling across the border.

In the 1940's a young Mexican boy came up with an idea to boost sales – the "worm in the bottle." Contrary to popular myth, the worm was simply a marketing ploy, and was never a Mexican tradition. Who knew the boy was such a visionary? Here, more then 60 years later, many people still think that <u>every</u> bottle of tequila has a worm in it. And in bars from coast to coast, the debate continues… What really killed the worm, and are you supposed to eat it?

While very few tequila bottles still come with worms in them, some brands of mescal are regularly bottled with butterfly caterpillars (not worms). There are two types, a red caterpillar and a white one. Of the two, the red is most prized, and folklore tells of aphrodisiac properties associated with it. These caterpillars are considered a delicacy in Mexico and are often sold as a common food item in the village markets. Although the Mescal Caterpillars do not really possess any magical properties, they are normally eaten, with salt and limes, as a tasty treat.

## Sources

"Brief history of what a tequila drink is.," *PageWise, Inc.*, 2002, <http://wvwv.essortment.com/ whattequiladri_rdvx.htm>, (5 April 2004).

Ian Chadwick, "From ancient pulque to today. Tequila's history and culture.," *The Cultured Traveler*, Volume 6, February 2004, <http://www.theculturedtraveler.com/ Archives/Feb2004/ Tequila.htm>, (4 April 2004).

Joseph A. Tyson, "Tequila - The Essence of Mexico," *Los Cabos Magazine - Los Cabos Visitor's Guide,* <http://www.loscabos guide.com/tequila/tequila-history.htm>, (3 April 2004).

"Tequila Mexico," *Mission Liquor and Tobacco,* 2003, <http://www.missionliquors.com/tequila/mexico-tequila.html>, (28 March 2004).

# Vodka

Vodka is a hard liquor produced from a variety of grains, and sometimes vegetables, such as potatoes. It is known for having a high proof (alcohol content) and virtually no flavor. This lack of distinctive flavor makes vodka especially easy to mix with other liqueurs, fruits and syrups.

Vodka, is the affectionate term for Voda (Russian for water), and indeed, is known in Russia as the "Little Water of Life." Vodka has its' roots firmly based in the cultures and traditions of not only Russia, but also Poland and Sweden.

## A Little History of Vodka

In the early 12th Century, the Russians began distilling rye vodka. It was a rather rough blend, with a significant alcohol kick. Honey was added about 300 years later, when found to mellow the flavor.

In the 1800's charcoal was discovered as a means of filtering out impurities. Up to this point, rye was the main grain used. Although variations were introduced from other countries, including spice and herb combinations, and vodka made from wheat and potatoes, rye was still considered to produce the best flavor.

Just as England had faced problems of alcohol abuse, and the disintegration of the community and economy due to alcohol consumption, so did Russia.

At the same time the United States was dealing with Prohibition, so too was Russia, (to a lesser extent). In 1917, the Russian government passed laws to ban all sales of vodka in public. From 1917 until 1936, no liquors with more then 20% alcohol (40 proof) were allowed to be sold.

The people became so depressed that the bans were lifted. Almost immediately, drunkenness took over again. Next, taxes were raised in an effort to curb the vodka sales. As a result, the distilleries went underground, creating a mixture called Samogon, meaning "self-brew."

Some of the companies that have developed out of the growth of Vodka's history include Smirnoff (Russia), Absolut (Sweden) and Polmos (Poland).

## Sources

Brian Smith, "The history of vodka," *PageWise, Inc.*, 2001, <http://txtx.essortment.com/vodkadrinks_rbov.htm>, (14 April 2004).

Mariab Hanik, "History of Vodka, origin, name and distilling in Poland," <http://www.polishvodka.com.pl/ history-vodka/title-page.htm>, (3 April 2004).

Michael Prokaziuk, "Vodka: From Peter the Great to Peter the Polluted," *Pimp Works*, <http://www.pimp works.org/~vincent /historymain.html#vodka>, (15 April 2004).

Paul Richardson and Mikhail Ivanov, "The Little Water of Life," *Vodkaphiles (sponsored by Russian Life magazine),* http://www.vodkaphiles.com/vodhis1.cfm, (3 May 2004).

"The History of Vodka," *Synertech International Corp.*, (a note on the website lists the original source as Nicholas Faith & Ian Wisniewski, Classic Vodka, 1997), <http://www.ivodka.com/ history.html>, (5 April 2004).

# Whiskey

Whiskey is a distilled liquor made from primarily from grains such as corn, rye, wheat and barley.

- **Aging** - the process of allowing whiskey to rest and settle. Aging is commonly done in new, used, charred or uncharred, oak barrels, and takes between two and thirty years to complete.

  The distinctive golden color of whiskey is the result of the natural chemical reaction between the alcohol and acids in the oak.

- **American Whiskey** - Whiskey distilled in the United States.

- **Blended** - Whiskey made from several other whiskeys and spirits.

- **Bourbon** - Whiskey distilled from no less then 51% corn, and specifically produced in Bourbon County, Kentucky.

- **Canadian Whiskey** - Whiskey distilled in Canada.

- **Corn Whiskey** - Whiskey made with at least 80% corn.

- **Irish Whiskey** - Whiskey distilled in Ireland, following Irish recipes and customs. Irish whiskeys are aged for a minimum of three years, and are distilled three separate times, resulting in an exceptionally smooth flavor.

  Irish whiskeys are often denoted as blended by a Catholic or Protestant distillery. Two of the most popular are Bushmill's and Jameson's.

- **Rye Whiskey** - Whiskey made with at least 51% rye.

- **Scotch Whiskey** - Whiskey distilled in Scotland, following Scottish recipes and customs, and aged a minimum of three years.

  There are four main areas in Scotland where whiskey is produced, including the Highlands and Lowlands.

  Many Scotch Whiskeys are named after the geographical area where they have been distilled, such as Glenlivet, Glenmorangie, Highland Park, and Longmorn.

- **Straight** - Whiskey which is not blended with other whiskeys.

- **Tennessee Whiskey** - Whiskey produced in Tennessee. One of the most popular is Jack Daniel's.

## Sources

Dr. Andreas Sorgatz, "A Glossary of Whiskey Terms…," *Sci-Face, Inc.* <http://math-www.uni-paderborn.de/~andi/WHISKY/ glossary.shtml>, (5 May 2004).

Dr. Andreas Sorgatz, "My Whiskey Notes…," *Sci-Face, Inc.* <http://math-www.uni-paderborn.de/~andi/ WHISKY/NOTE/index.shtml>, (5 May 2004).
**This page contains the most complete listing of Scotch whiskies I have found, and is an excellent resource.**

"Whiskey Terms & Definitions," *kc.rr.com/mashbill*, <http://home.kc.rr.com/mashbill/ whiskey_terms.htm>, (28 April 2004).

# Wines

- **White Wine** - A light, slightly sweet, fruity wine, made from either red or white grapes. The skins are removed prior to fermentation, giving these wines a lighter flavor then a blush or red wine.

   The color of a white wine may range from clear to a soft gold. The golden color comes from aging the wine in oak barrels. The longer the wine is stored in contact with the oak, the darker the golden color.

   White wines are most commonly served with light foods, such as shrimp, crab, lobster, grilled fish, cheese, appetizers, salads, chicken, game hens, turkey, duck, goose, pork and veal. White wines should be served chilled.

White wines often take their names from the types of grapes used. For example, Zinfandel wine made from Zinfandel grapes.

Popular white wines include Johannesburg Riesling, Chablis, Pinot Grigio, Chardonney, Cabernet Blanc, and Gewurztraminer, a premium white wine with a flavor that is similar to grapefruit and roses.

- **Blush Wine** - A light, flavorful wine made from red grapes. The skins are left on for a short period of time during the fermentation process, giving these wines a distinctive light pink color.

    Blush wines are most commonly served with light meals or brunch. Some of the best foods to pair with these wines are cheese, various appetizers, shellfish such as clams, mussels, lobster, crab, shrimp and oysters. Creamy pasta dishes and light meats such as chicken, veal, and pork are also good with these wines. Blush wines are best served chilled.

    Popular blush wines include Rosè, Vin Rosè, White Zinfandel, and White Merlot.

- **Red Wine** - A full-bodied wine made from whole red grapes, including the skins.

    Red wines are commonly part of the evening meal, and are traditionally served at room temperature.

    Some reds, such as Burgundy, make particularly good cooking wines. Others, such as Merlot, Shiraz and Chianti, are often enjoyed as sipping wines. Cabernet Sauvignon is excellent served with fresh strawberries and chocolate, or my personal favorite, peanut butter and crackers.

    Full bodied reds pair well with red sauce pasta dishes such as lasagna and cannelloni. Some red wines provide a wonderful compliment to beef, lamb, and salmon, while others pair better with game birds such as a pheasant, duck or goose.

Use care when mixing strong red wines, especially Burgundy, with aged cheeses. This combination can sometimes result in heart palpitations.

Some of the most popular red wines include Sherry, Cabernet Sauvignon, Burgundy, Chianti, Paisano, Shiraz, and Merlot.

Unlike white wines where the name reflects the type of grapes used, red wines are more commonly named for the region the grapes are grown in. For example, Burgundy made with grapes from Burgundy, France.

- **Dessert Wine** -Red wines that have been fortified with brandy. These wines generally have a higher alcohol content then most red wines, and a very sweet flavor.

   Dessert wines are often served with fruits, pie or cake. Some people prefer them as a sipping wine. As with other reds, serve dessert wines at room temperature

   Port wine is a popular dessert wine, which was originally developed in Portugal. Other popular dessert wines include Ruby Port, Madeira, Marsala and Sweet Sherry, a dessert wine with a distinctive, slightly nutty, flavor.

- **Sparkling Wine** - A sweet and very bubbly white or blush wine. These wines are known for their effervescence, a good example is Champagne.

   Sparkling wines are often served at celebrations, and make a wonderful addition to the brunch table. Best foods to complement these wines are breakfast type dishes, light salads, appetizers, and desserts such as cake, pie and fruits. As with the other white and blush wines, serve sparkling wines chilled.

   While some sparkling wines take their name from the type of grapes used, such as Champagne, made from Champagne grapes, others do not follow that pattern.

   Besides Champagne, other popular sparkling wines include Cold Duck and Sparkling Rosè.

- **Kosher Wine** - Wine that has been made in accordance with Jewish customs. These wines are blessed by a Rabbi, and are usually made from Concord grapes. Manischevitz is one of the best known brands.

- **Flavored or Fruit Wine** - Wine typically made from a white or blush wine which have had fruit extracts, syrups, and/or artificial flavors added.

   Unlike dessert wines, flavored wines are not fortified with brandy. These popular drinking wines are often packaged in small quantities and sold as "wine coolers." As with other white and blush wines, these wines are best served chilled.

## Sources

"Common Wine Questions," *Gallo of Sonoma*, <http://www.gallo ofsonoma.com/wine_questions.asp>, (28 April 2004).

Dan Clarke, "Tasting History, A Trip into Inglenook's Past," *California Wine and Food Magazine*, <http://www.californiawine andfood.com/wine/ inglenook-tasting.htm>, (28 April 2004).

"Guide to Food and Wine Pairing," *Chateau Ste. Michelle Winery*, <http://www.ste-michelle.com/ Sub_TraditionalPairings.cfm?>, (2 May 2004).

"Our Wines," *Gossamer Bay Vineyards*, <http://www.gossamer bay.com/wines.html>, (21 April 2004)

"Wine Basics," *Almaden Vineyards*, <http://www. almaden.com/ winebasics/whatsinthewine.htm>, (24 April 2004).

---

A few drops of Bitters mixed in Ginger Ale, Coke, or 7-Up will help stop morning sickness and motion sickness, and are good for calming upset stomachs.

# Is That a Ghost in Your Pocket?
## Or Are You Just Happy to See Me?

Tacoma, Washington is a city with an intriguing history, and many secrets. Built in the shadow of Seattle, Tacoma grew and flourished during the early days of the West. As a major seaport, Tacoma became a fertile ground for legends, myths, and of course, ghost stories.

Here is one for you, of a little bar in South Tacoma. Is this story true? You decide. I can only tell you what I experienced, and relay the story as it was told to me.

One night while cleaning up, I heard the sounds of a woman's high heels sharply clicking as she walked across the marble floor. The bar had been closed for over an hour, and I was the only one there. My first concern was that I might have accidentally locked someone in. Immediately following was the disturbing notion that someone might have been hiding, waiting for a chance to rob me.

Bravery can only take you so far, I thought, as I glanced about for something to use as a weapon. Finding an old baseball bat, I casually strolled around the poolroom and kitchen. The doors were still locked from the inside. I even checked the bathrooms. No one. Puzzled, I stood in the middle of the dance floor and made a slow survey of the room.

Moonlight streaming through the windows softly illuminated the foyer and antique bar. The ancient brick walls with their weathered reds and browns, created a cozy and intimate setting.

I had always liked working here. For some reason, even when working late, I never felt alone. Laughing at myself, and my vivid imagination, I turned to go back to work.

But, just as I started to relax, the footsteps started again.

It sounded as if someone was walking towards me. There was a sudden rush of cold air, and I clearly heard a woman's voice say, "Uh, oh." Then, nothing more.

I asked the owner about it the next day. According to her, the building had been a nightclub in the early 1900's. It had been a roaring hot spot. The place to see, and be seen by the wealthy and flamboyant of the Tacoma uppercrust.

During Prohibition, the nightclub became a Speak Easy, a secret club that served blackmarket liquor. To gain admittance, you had to *speak easy*, (whisper the password) through a little slot opened in the heavily fortified door. Only the most exclusive members of society were given the secret password.

Boasting to have the best in bootleg liquor and wild women the club flourished. Patrons came in droves, undeterred by the escalating violence of the times. For many, the threat of a police raid added spice to the clandestine poker games, and a seductive flavor to the illegal whiskey. Times were hard, and club became more and more popular, until one night when a horrific gunfight erupted.

No one knows who started it, or why. Maybe it was the rigged card games or a fight over a woman. Whatever happened, the reaction to the first shot was instantaneous.

Chairs were thrown across the room, and tables were overturned, as everyone dove for safety. Since most men and many women of that time carried guns, what had started as a single shot, became a blaze of bullets as people frantically fired in self-defense.

Women screamed as bullets strafing the bar's 30 foot mirror, sent glass shards flying like shrapnel. Stray bullets hit the ceiling supports bringing the chandeliers crashing down. Plunged into darkness, panic took hold. Hysterical patrons dashed into the streets, running for their cars. Honking horns and squealing tires marked their hasty escape.

Within minutes the streets were deserted, and an uneasy hush descended. Out of the shadows came men with hammers and nails. They worked swiftly, boarding up the doors and windows.

An hour later, the building was completely closed down, and not a single person remained.

Later, as the clouds drifted away, light from the moon glittered on the broken glass littering the parking lot. From a distance, it almost seemed as if they deliberately illuminated several nails accidentally dropped in the grass. In the distant, a church bell rang. Then, there was only silence.

Rumors started soon after that night. People walking by heard laughter, music, and voices, coming from the deserted structure, and flickers of light were often seen though the boarded up windows. The locals avoided the building, saying it was haunted. Even the bums would cross the street rather then come too close.

The nightclub remained boarded shut for many years, until a real estate company tried to lease the building. But, strange things were afoot. Agents showing the property complained about doors that slammed shut by themselves, lights that flickered off and on, and bits of ceiling material that fell on them for no apparent reason.

The nightclub had been closed so suddenly, that the kitchen still held many serving dishes and dinner plates. It was not uncommon to hear dishes crashing against the walls, as if hurled by an unseen hand. The broken crockery occasionally sliding across the dance floor, to rest at the potential tenant's feet.

In the late 1940's, the property was sold, and the new owner began renovations. While working, the construction crew discovered a hidden closet. There, under piles of debris, lay several bodies. They were twisted and dry, virtually mummified in the airless room. One body was that of a young woman, wearing high heels. Her tattered clothing was covered with what appeared to be dried blood.

According to the story, the murders were never solved. In fact, the identities of the people were never known. Did they die that night in the gunfight? Or had they been stashed there, victims of a previous crime?

In 1950, the club reopened as a restaurant, under the name *Steve's Gay Nineties*.

All looked rosy for the club, but behind the scenes, the reports of unexplained activity continued. In 1977, the restaurant was closed, and the building was again boarded shut.

The site remained undisturbed for nearly 25 years, until opening as a sports bar, in late 2001. The ghosts immediately made their presence known.

No one has ever solved the question of what to do about the hauntings. Many nights, I heard voices, laughter, the clicking of high heels, and the sounds of music. Books fell off the shelves for no reason. Calculators, cell phones and corkscrews would vanish, only to reappear in another room. We lost a good cook when the mischievous spirits threw dishes at him, and countless customers reported seeing faces in the mirrors when no one was there.

Apparently for some, the party is still going on. Which goes to show you that those who are pranksters in life will probably continue long after.

Would I work in another building full of ghosts? Sure. My only question is this, are they good tippers?

More information on *Steve's Gay Nineties* can be found on the following websites:

Joe Thompson, "Steve's Gay '90s (Tacoma)," *Cable Car Lines in the Pacific Northwest*, <www.cable-car-guy.com/html/ccsea.html#steves>, (28 April 2004).

"Steve's Gay 90's Restaurant," *Puget Sound Pipeline Online*, <www.pstos.org/instruments/wa/tacoma/ gay90s.htm>, (21 April 2004).

# The Business of Bartending

In some ways, bartending is a very strange profession. Since bartending jobs are relatively easy to find, bartenders tend to be somewhat transient. In other words, bartenders move around, a LOT. Why? Better money, better hours, friends, location, there are many reasons. All of this is good news for you. Because bartenders and cocktail servers change jobs often, there are always new positions opening up. A bar may not be hiring this morning, but they may be tonight. Or, a nightclub may not be hiring bartenders, but you can get on as a cocktail server, and in a few days – Viola! A bartending job opens up.

There is nothing wrong with starting as a server, and moving up. Servers can make very good money, and many places will want to start you cocktailing so they can see how well you interact with the customers. My advice? Go for it.

What is a cocktailer? Cocktailers, are different from a restaurant waitress or waiter. While they may serve food, the majority of the time they ferry drink orders to the bar, pick up the drinks (after the bartender makes them), and deliver them to the customer (keeping the tip). A good cocktailer can actually make more then the bartender in tips. The friendlier you are, and the more you SMILE, the more tips you will make.

There are several ways to make money as a bartender or a server. Serving liquor and food, providing exceptional customer service, and gambling tips from casino tables or pull tab players.

At the end of the night, the servers "tip-out" the bartender. Usually a tip-out is about 10% of what the server has earned in tips from liquor sales.

# Money, Money, Money

## How much does a bartender make?

Let me hit you with the "sticker shock" right away. Bartenders are normally paid minimum wage. Yikes! At first, that sounds scary. But take heart. The majority of your income comes from tips. Your hourly salary is only a small part of the money you earn.

An average bartender can earn $100-$300 per night in tips on weeknights, and $200-$500 on weekends. Several factors determine how much money you can make. The most important is foot traffic. The more people you have coming and going, the more opportunities you have to earn tips. For this reason, a bartender can make equally good money working in a nightclub, an expensive restaurant, or a busy neighborhood bar and grill.

For convenience, let us say the minimum wage in your state is $7.00/hr, and you work an 8-hour shift.

1. You are new, and the night is fairly slow, or you have a day shift and you make **$80 in tips**.
   Wages ($ 7.00/hr) + Tips ($10.00/hr) = **$17.00/hr**

2. You get a better shift, and your tips increase to **$160**.
   Wages ($ 7.00/hr) + Tips ($20.00/hr) = **$27.00/hr**

3. You get a weekend shift, and your tips increase to **$320**.
   Wages ($ 7.00/hr) + Tips ($40.00/hr) = **$47.00/hr**

Some people prefer working in a job with a steady paycheck. For me, I prefer working for tips. One reason is that I take home cash at the end of every shift. No more waiting two or three weeks for a paycheck. Work this weekend, and pay the rent on Monday. It is a wonderful feeling to have cash in your pocket.

In bartending your attitude counts for a lot. If you are working hard, providing good customer service, smiling, and acting in a positive, friendly manner, you will usually make very good money. A new bartender that knows only a few drinks, but has a great attitude, will usually make great tips. On the other hand, a bartender with years of experience and a grouchy attitude will make much less.

Bartenders not only make tips on alcohol and food service, but also casino type games, such as pull-tabs. Customers will generally pay the bartender a percentage of their winnings. On a $500 winner, you may be tipped $25 to $100, just for pulling the ticket. Many times I have made $300-$400 in a single shift, on pull-tabs tips alone.

Gamblers will often come into a bar when it is slower, because they know you will have more time for them. So don't despair if you are scheduled to work on a weekend day shift, or on a slow night. Just roll up your sleeves and get ready to play. No, I don't mean actually gamboling with them. I am talking about having fun with your customers.

Cheer the players on when they get a winner, and show real excitement when they open their tickets. Since half the excitement of pull-tabs is playing with the bartender, when customers find out how much fun you are, they will start coming in during your shifts. Before long, you will be very busy with pull-tab players.

There are many ways to help make your bartending career fun and lucrative. Ultimately, you are the biggest factor. Bartending is one career where you really do control your destiny.

# Increasing Your Income

- **Be FRIENDLY** – Have fun with your customers and let them know you are glad they have come by.

- Get to know as many customers by name as possible, and try to remember what they like to drink.

- To increase your customer volume, invite customers back when you will be working. Simply say, "Hey, I am working again Friday night from 6 p.m. to close. I hope you can come by." This helps customer's feel wanted and special. You may be surprised how quickly your shifts will pick up in sales and tips.

- **Don't Flirt Too Much** – Have fun with customers, but don't use the bar as your private pick-up place. Spending too much time with one customer will leave others feeling left out and may make them angry. Being too suggestive with customers may make them feel uncomfortable, and can even lead to complaints.

- **Don't Solve Their Problems** – Remember that people go to bars to relax, vent frustrations and meet other people in a casual social environment. If a customer talks to you about their personal problems, depending how busy you are, you may be able to listen, but don't try to give advice. Be sympathetic, but uninvolved.

- **Don't Expect Customers to Solve Your Problems.** People go to bars to relax, not be your personal counselor. Leave your problems at home. Come in with a good attitude, and a big smile. Your tips will be a direct reflection of how you come across to others. Many people don't realize that they could significantly increase tips by being friendlier and *SMILING* more.

- **<u>Selective Memory</u>** – Customers will say all kinds of things to you, and you will see them act in ways that they may not want anyone to remember. When in doubt, play dumb. Act as if nothing has happened, and you don't remember anything said to you. A customer that was obnoxious to you last night may be sweet as can be today. And a man that came in with the blond girl yesterday may show up with his <u>wife</u> today.

## Finding a Job

### Where should I Start?

1. Bars
2. Restaurants with a bar or lounge
3. Hotels
4. Nightclubs
5. Taverns
6. Casinos
7. Country Clubs, especially in the summer
8. Ski Lodges, many operate year-round
9. Resorts
10. Airport Lounges
11. Breweries
12. Wineries
13. Strip Clubs, if they serve alcohol.
14. Private Catering Companies
15, Trade Show Companies
16, Large Convention Halls
17. Wedding Planners
18. Marinas
19. Places that host company parties and events
20. Places that host weddings and celebrations
21. Newspapers
22. Internet
23. Chamber of Commerce meetings

24.    Network with friends and coworkers
25.    Stop in at places you would like to work and get to know the bar manager.
26.    Beer salesmen.
27.    Bar and restaurant supply stores.
28.    Bar and restaurant supply salesmen.
29.    Friends
30.    Family
31.    Local magazines and publications. Such as
    a.  Gambler Today
    b.  The Stranger
    c.  Around the Sound
    d.  Northwest Nightclubs

## **Other Helpful Hints**

- Only about 10% of the jobs available are listed in the paper. Go to several bars in an area you would like to work and ask if they have openings. Don't expect to hear back on a resume you sent in. Go talk to the managers face to face whenever possible.

- Don't stop at one. Interview with several establishments. Multiple bars may want to hire you at the same time.

- Check local newspapers first thing in the morning, or on-line, to get a jump on other job seekers. Bar managers tend to hire the first person they like, so don't wait until after lunch to pursue an ad you saw in the paper. **\*Dress for success\*** Go to the interview ***ready to start work in an hour!***

- Be persistent. Show the manager you really want the job.

- For the best success, avoid calling or trying to meet with the bar manager during peak times - lunch rush (11 a.m. to 2 p.m.), or dinner rushes (4 p.m. to 7 p.m.).

- **Don't call about a job if you have been drinking.** You will not be quick with your answers, and you may say things that are very inappropriate.

- Don't try to get on the manager's good side by putting down the other employees.

- Be friendly, **but <u>do not</u> flirt with the manager to get an interview.**

## Can You Start Tonight?
### How to Ace the Interview

Bar manager have very little time, too much to do, and 1000 other things pulling their attention away from the excitement of interviewing yet another bartender. This is beneficial to you, because bar managers tend to make decisions quickly so they can get back to work. Knowing this, strive to make a very strong, positive initial impression followed by a short, sweet interview and an immediate job offer.

Here are two big tips:

# SMILE

Walk into the interview with excitement, show enthusiasm, and flash a big smile. Did you notice I said "smile" again? It is surprising how many people are in the habit of looking grumpy and resentful. Bartending is a very social job, in a party atmosphere. You need to look and act, like you are enjoying yourself.

# Act like you have a pulse.

Do you walk around full of energy, or moving as slowly as possible? If your normal speed resembles that of a turtle, then pick up the pace and get with the program. Show some energy act like you are happy, full of life and ready to take on the world.

Besides wanting to get the job, you have an image to uphold. Bartenders have the reputation of being energetic, easy going, full of fun, always on the run, and great partiers.

Bartenders are also known for possessing incredible amounts of absolutely useless trivia. If you are trivia- challenged, don't worry. Within a month you will have more quips, jokes, useless facts, and bad pick up lines up your sleeve then you ever thought possible.

Once the manager determines you are indeed alive and reasonably friendly, there are a few key items he will want to know about you. He may not ask these questions directly, but rather, base a hiring decision on his overall impression of you. Be ready to answer questions with lots of energy and friendly, smiling facial expressions.

- **Will my customers like you?** (Will I get complements or complaints?)

- **Are you friendly?** Positive? Outgoing? (This is no time to be shy.)

- Can you perform the job responsibilities quickly and efficiently?

- If you need training, will you learn quickly, or fight me the whole way?

- Will you make us money?

- **Will you be *reliable*?** (Not calling in sick, showing up on time, etc.)

- Will I like working with you?

- Will the other bar staff like you?

## For the interview, arrive early, and bring:

1. A pen.

2. A list of 2-3 <u>current</u> references, including names and phone numbers. It is a good idea to contact your references ahead of time and make sure that they remember who you are, and are willing to be a reference for you.

   **If you have been fired from a job <u>don't include that person as a reference!</u>**

3. A resume, if you have one.

4. Your driver's license or state ID card.

5. Not a US citizen? Be sure to bring proof you are legal to work in this country.

6. Social security card.

7. Copies of your Food Handler's permit. Never give out your originals.

8. Copies of your state required licenses. Never give out your originals.

- **<u>Don't prejudge an establishment.</u>** A bar that looks run down may be very busy and have a great crowd. Go to every interview. And always do your best.

- **<u>Go to the interview alone</u>**. Nothing says, "Hi, I'm incompetent," like taking your mother or boyfriend to an interview with you.

- **<u>Dress for success.</u>** Call ahead, or visit the bar before your interview. Notice what the bartender is wearing. All black? Black pants or skirt and a white top? Try to follow that dress code. It lets the interviewer know you are ready to start work <u>TODAY</u>. Many times you may apply for a job and start working an hour later.

# Keeping Your Boss Happy

- **Bar Time** – Most bars have their clocks set 15-20 minutes ahead. This is to allow a little extra time to clear the bar of customers at 2 am, without being in violation of the state liquor serving laws. ** Note to remember: The bar will schedule your shifts based on BAR TIME, so be sure to set your watch ahead to match it, or you will be late for work.

- Arrive for work at least 20 minutes early for your shift. If you are going to be late, even 5 minutes call and talk to a <u>supervisor</u>.

- Arrive for work in clean, neat clothing. Be sure to follow your bars' dress or uniform code.

- Always be personally clean. Shower regularly, wash your hair, and keep beards neat and trimmed. *Brush your teeth. And, use mouthwash as needed.

- **Shoes** – I recommend good quality black or white (depending on the bar's dress code), tennis shoes or other athletic shoes. It is easy to slip or twist an ankle in high heels. Also, you want to be able to show the bar manager you are FAST and efficient. No open toed shoes, they are in violation of Labor and Industries laws. Wear shoes that are comfortable. You may be on your feet for the next 8-12 hours.

- **Earrings** – Keep them small. Dangling or hoop earrings tend to get lost, or caught in your hair and can be distracting (not to mention painful).

- **Make-Up** – Wear it according to the bar's standards. A conservative, upscale restaurant might not appreciate a male bartender wearing eyeliner and lipstick – while a trendy nightclub would think it was great. Girls – don't overdo, keep it simple and easy to repair. You might not get a break for several hours. Makeup that needs to be "touched up" every 15 minutes will not be your friend. Most customers seem to really appreciate a clean, neat appearance.

- **Hair** – It should be CLEAN. Keep it simple and neat. If you have long hair, wear it in a way that looks professional, or even a little sexy – but is out of your way, so that you do not need to constantly push it back in place or play with it. Customers do not like to see their bartender or server playing with their hair, and then serving them food. A good trick is to use a little mousse or styling gel before work. A quick brush with a little water and it will stay put for hours.

- **Socks** – Wear socks that match your pants or skirt. Don't mess up by wearing white socks with black pants.

- Avoid smoking, eating, or drinking beverages behind the bar while you are working. Step outside the bar serving area when you take a break or get a drink.

- Always wash your hands after eating, using the restroom, clearing dirty dishes, and <u>cleaning ashtrays</u>. Not only is this a health requirement, but it will also help keep you from catching customers' colds and flu.

- Never drink alcohol while working. Any alcohol you consume should be completely out of your system before you start work. Coffee, water, juice and soft drinks are normally available continuously at no charge while you are working.

- Don't show up for work "high," drunk, or hung over.

- Be careful about drinking or partying in the place you work. Remember: if you drink too much and act too wild, it could affect your job status. Also, if you stay out late drinking, your boss will definitely know why you are calling in sick the next day. It is also possible to say things, or act in ways with coworkers, which you would not normally do if you were not drinking.

- **No Gambling** – Not even on the SuperBowl. Many bars prohibit employees who draw pull-tabs for customers from playing the pull-tabs themselves (even off duty). Involvement in side bets, or illegal bar wagers, can cost you your Permit to Serve, and may get the bar in trouble with the state gambling commission.

- You may not have a secure place to keep your purse or wallet while working. Carry important licenses and any cash in your pocket. Never leave keys, cash, or credit cards in your wallet or purse, if you can't watch it.

- NEVER, EVER, tell anyone how much you make in tips. This includes customers. If a coworker asks, simply say, "I did OK," or "It was a good night." Leave a positive impression that you are satisfied, but give no information. Nothing will make enemies faster then coworkers thinking you make more in tips then they do. Even if it is true.

- Don't count your tips while at work – simply exchange any small change (quarters, dimes, etc.), casino chips (if you have any), and put all the rest of the dollar bills in a bag and don't look at it again until you get home. DO NOT LET IT OUT OF YOUR HANDS. Setting down a bag of cash while you use the restroom or talk to a friend is an open invitation to lose it. No counting tips at work. Don't be fooled into thinking people are not watching you and counting with you. And you would be surprised how fast everyone that works with you will know how much money you made that night.

- Flashing money as you count your tips can make you a target for robbery. Also avoid counting your tips in your car while in the parking lot. Remember – a lot of people may have watched you walk out with $200-$500 in cash.

# What Liquor Serving Laws Mean to You

It is important to stress the following points. You, as a bartender have a significant amount of responsibility to make sure your patrons enjoy themselves in a safe and legal manner.

## <u>Bartending is a fun and exciting career.</u>

<u>Always</u> remember to serve responsibly.

Good bartenders don't let their customers drive drunk.

It's up to <u>you</u> to say "when."

Know your State's legal drinking age,
and never serve to a minor.

This chapter is based on the training materials used to qualify individuals for the Permit to Serve Alcohol (commonly called the Mixology or Bartender License), for the state of Washington.

This chapter contains general information and is not intended to be all-inclusive. Please check with your manager or local liquor board for laws that apply to your particular state or city.

## Never Over Serve

For most states, it is illegal to serve a person who is obviously intoxicated. This means, if the person walks into your bar, and they have already had too much, you <u>cannot legally</u> serve him/her. Not even one drink. Coffee, soda, other <u>non-alcoholic</u> drinks can, and should be encouraged.

Should the person leave? Most of the time, there is no reason for them to leave your bar, as long as he/she is:

1. Not acting in a manner that is dangerous to others (such as picking fights, hitting people, or making threats).

2. Not sleeping. People in your bar must remain AWAKE.

3. Not acting obnoxious, cussing, throwing things, or in general, making you and everyone else crazy.

4. Keeping their clothes on.

Try to prevent anyone who is drunk from leaving, especially if they will be driving. Offer to call a cab, call a friend, or one of their family members. Try to get the person to eat something, or have some coffee.

## Serving Facts to Keep in Mind

**A 12-ounce bottle of beer, a 6-ounce glass of wine, and a 1-ounce shot of 86 proof liquor all contain about the same amount of alcohol.**

Does that surprise you? Most people *assume* that beer and wine have lower alcohol contents then "hard" liquor.

1. *Anyone* can become intoxicated on *any* liquor – if they drink enough of it.

2. Factors that can cause one person to become intoxicated faster then another can include:

a.  **Weight**. Heavier or overweight people are often able to drink more then a slender person before exhibiting signs of intoxication.

b.  **Gender**. Women tend to become intoxicated faster then men, on less alcohol.

c.  **Muscle mass**. The more muscular the person, the more they can generally drink before showing signs of intoxication.

d.  **How long since their last meal**. Food slows down the absorption of alcohol by the body, allowing a person to drink more, without showing signs of intoxication.

3.  The average person can process about **1 ounce of hard liquor an hour.**

---

**Only TIME will allow a person to sober up.**
**Coffee and fresh air can <u>wake the person up</u>,**
**but only TIME will allow the alcohol**
**to process out of their body.**

---

## How Can You Tell if Someone is Drunk?

Follow the **<u>PuBS</u>** rule:

1.  **<u>Physical changes</u>** – Watch for stumbling, dropping things, unablity to count change, lighting the wrong end of the cigarette, knocking over drinks, glassy eyes, etc.

2.  **<u>Behavioral changes</u>** – While some people become moody and withdrawn, other become loud, boisterous, or even violent. Some may start picking fights, complaining about their friends, or the service they are receiving.

3. <u>**Speech**</u> – Are they slurring their words, forgetting what they are talking about, or talking in a rambling and nonsensical manner?

4. <u>**And the "U"?**</u> That stands for YOU, using good judgment and common sense.

Not everyone will show <u>every</u> symptom. But, virtually everyone will show at least one <u>or more</u>. If in doubt, you will need to use your own judgment. Try to watch how many drinks a person is consuming, and in what period of time. Especially watch out for doubles and "high octane" drinks like Exotics and Long Island Ice Teas – which have 2 to 2-1/2 ounces of liquor in each one. Exotics taste good, and people often drink them quickly without realizing how much liquor they have consumed.

Remember: **There is a time lag from the time a person consumes the drink, until they start exhibiting signs of intoxication.** This is why a person can drink a couple of shots in the car, walk into your bar, have a cup of coffee, and fall off the barstool. The liquor simply needed time to catch up.

## Cutting Someone Off

When you have determined that a person needs to be "cut off" (not served any more liquor for that day), here are some helpful rules to follow:

1. <u>**Never back down.**</u> Be firm, but polite, and offer other non-alcoholic beverages and food. Be hospitable and friendly, but stand your ground.

2. <u>**Alert other servers.**</u> Often a person that has been cut off will try to get a drink from other servers or other patrons.

3. **<u>Avoid getting into an argument</u>.** Stay calm, and avoid comments, generalizations, name-calling or making remarks that could be inflammatory, especially comments regarding gender, race or a person's parentage.

4. **<u>Gossip</u>:** Avoid talking about that person behind their back to other patrons.

5. **<u>Refer to posted signs</u>.** If your bar has signs posted stating "it is illegal to serve someone who is intoxicated," point to those signs and use that as a way to back up what you are saying.

6. **<u>Cameras</u>:** Simply remind the customer that everything that happens is being recorded. This also works well to help control drug dealing in your bar.

## Drinking and Driving

Know your state's laws regarding drinking and driving, including the blood alcohol levels for DUI and other possible legal infractions. In the State of Washington, the BAC (Blood Alcohol Concentration) for a DUI "Driving Under the Influence," conviction is .08, and .05 for "Driving While Impaired."

Statistically, people with a BAC of .05 or higher have a 300-400% higher risk of being involved in an accident.

In the state of Washington an average of 280 people a year die in alcohol related accidents. For every person that dies, five others are injured.

If a person you served leaves your bar and is involved in an accident, both you and the bar can be held liable. It is called **Third Party Liability**.

# Minors

**It is illegal to serve minors alcohol**. Know your state's drinking age, and follow it. You can be held criminally responsible if you are caught serving a minor. This carries even more impact when you consider that **10-20% of the traffic accidents involving alcohol are caused by underage drinkers.**

# Drinking and Drugs

Using drugs with alcohol can compound (increase) the effect of the drug. This is true regardless if the drugs are prescription, over the counter or illegal street drugs. It is possible for very dangerous and toxic reactions to occur.

Mixing antihistamine, commonly taken for allergies, with alcohol can be dangerous. Many cold remedies say they help you feel better and get a good night's sleep. Ever tried one? They can knock you out for a couple days. While this is great to help you get over a cold, it can be dangerous if you are driving. Take a look at the label, you will find <u>alcohol and antihistamine</u>.

Decongestants can make a person sick to their stomach when mixed with alcohol, especially red wines.

Some street drugs can be deadly when combined with alcohol. Be especially watchful for "club drugs," like Ecstasy.

Drugs that are <u>depressants</u> such as Marijuana, can make a person act much more depressed, "out of it," lost, or confused when mixed with alcohol.

Drugs that are <u>stimulants</u> such as Cocaine, can make a person extremely irritable, hyperactive, or edgy, and can cause extreme mood swings when mixed with even a slight amount of alcohol.

Although many people don't realize it, <u>alcohol is a depressant</u>. This explains why a person who is already upset may become much more so after a couple of drinks.

The exhilaration people sometimes feel when drinking is caused by the increased sugar to the system, and the effect alcohol has the brain's center of inhibition.

---

**The most common *depressant* in America is alcohol.
The most common *stimulant* is caffeine.**

---

## Alcohol and Pregnancy

In most states, it is ILLEGAL to refuse service to a pregnant woman, it is considered discrimination. You can make other suggestions, such as juice, coffee or a non-alcoholic drink, but you can't refuse to serve her, based on the pregnancy alone. Most states require signs to be posted alerting customers to the dangers of drinking while pregnant, including the risk of Fetal Alcohol Syndrome.

## Times of Service

Know your state's times to legally serve alcohol. Some jurisdictions may have different times. Be sure you check on this. For many states, 2 a.m. is the cut off, and service can start again at 6 a.m.

## Source:
Washington State Liquor Control Board, *Handbook for Liquor Licensees*, 2004.

## Notes to Keep Handy

I work in the State of: _____

The legal drinking age is: _____

The legal BAC for driving **IMPAIRED** is: _____

The legal BAC for driving **DRUNK** is: _____

I can serve liquor between the hours of:____ and ____

---

For burned on coffee in a glass pot – empty the pot, and allow it to cool. Fill the pot with 1/4" table salt; add 3 inches of ice cubes and about 2 ounces of soda water. Swirl, and let sit (alternately), until all the burned coffee is lifted off. Wash the pot as usual and it is ready to use again.

# Bartending Terms

- ***Absolut*** - A popular brand of Swedish vodka. Comes in a variety of flavors such as: Citron (lemon), Mandarin (orange) and Kurrent (blackberry).

- **Against the Wall** - A drink that is topped with 1/2 ounce of *Galliano*. For example, a *"Slow Screw against the wall."*

- ***Akvavit*** **(Aquavit)** - A caraway and rye flavored liquor, similar to vodka, commonly served in Scandinavian communities. It is best served chilled, with a beer chaser.

- **Amaretto** - An almond or cherry flavored liqueur. Amaretto is especially popular in coffee drinks.

- ***B&B*** - Brandy and Benedictine.

- **Back** - A drink on the side, such as coffee or Coke. Commonly referred to by the name of the side drink. For example, a *"coffee back"* or a *"Coke back."* The back is served so the patron can alternate between two drinks. Always offer a back with brandy, cognac, and straight shots.

   Customers are not normally charged for the back when it is served with an alcoholic drink, unless the back is also alcoholic. For example, a *"shot of whiskey with a beer back."* See also **Chaser.**

- **Bank** - A specific amount of money given to the bartender for the cash register. This cash is used for making change, and must be returned at the end of the shift.

- **Bar Back (Porter)** - A person who stocks the bar with ice, beer, liquors, and supplies. A good bar back is invaluable during rush times. Always remember to tip your bar back.

- **Bar Time** - Most bars have their clocks set 15-20 minutes ahead of the actual time. This allows a few extra minutes at closing time to clear the bar of customers, without being in violation of the state liquor serving laws.

  **The bar will schedule your shifts based on BAR TIME, so be sure to set your watch ahead to match it, or you will be late for work.**

- ***Benedictine*** - A liqueur with a strong herbal flavor, made from a variety of herbs and spices, including vanilla, nutmeg and cloves.

- **Bite Me** - A humorous term used when you want to swear at someone, but not come across with the same impact as using straight profanity. It is sort of the verbal equivalent of flipping someone off.

- **Bitters** - Syrup with a strong clove flavor, made from a combination of herbs and spices. Bitters are very strong, and are used to give an herbal flavor to some exotic drinks and an *"Old Fashioned."*

  Bitters also have medicinal value. A few drops on a lime wedge can help stop hiccups, and a few drops in Ginger Ale or Coke can help calm seasickness and morning sickness.

- **Blended** - A drink made in a blender. For example, a *"blended margarita."*

- **Blended** - A specific type of liquor made from a combination of similar liquors. For example, a *"blended whiskey."*

  A blended whiskey may be made up of as many as 75 different types of whiskey bases (80-125 proof) and spirits (liquors above 190 proof). Each whiskey base is aged a different amount of time. The final whiskey is built by layering the different bases and spirits and allowing them to combine over time. This combining process is known as aging.

- **Bourbon** - A special type of whiskey, made from at least 51% corn, and distilled in Bourbon County, Kentucky. Bourbon is stored in new charred barrels after distilling, and is aged at least 2 years.

- **Brandy** - Brandy is a special family of liquors. These liquors have an alcohol base, which comes from grape wine, and is often mixed with a variety of fruits and berries. The result is a very flavorful liquor that can be quite strong, sometimes as high as 84 proof.

  Brandies tend to be regional in production, based on the available fruits in the area.

  For the label to read *"Brandy,"* the liquor must be made solely from grapes. If other fruits are added, the type or types must be included in the label name, for example, *"Peach Brandy"* or *"Apricot Brandy."*

  Brandies are aged in oak barrels for 3-8 years.

- **Bruised** - A drink that has been shaken with ice, rather than stirred, and served in a chilled glass. This term usually refers to a Martini or a Manhattan.

- **Bucket** - A medium size, wide mouth glass that holds about 10 ounces of liquid.

- **Bud** - *Budweiser Beer*. A popular American beer.

- **CC** - *Canadian Club* whiskey. Also short for credit card.

- ***Chambord*** - A liqueur with a strong raspberry or grape flavor, used in making Grape Nehi's and Black Opals.

- **Chaser** - A drink on the side, such as coffee or Coke. Commonly referred to by the name of the side drink. For example, a *"coffee chaser"* or a *"Coke chaser."* The chaser is served so the patron can alternate between two drinks. Always offer a chaser with brandy, cognac, and straight shots.

  Customers are not normally charged for the chaser when it is served with an alcoholic drink, unless it is also alcoholic. For example, a *"shot of whiskey with a beer chaser."* The term "chaser" is more common in an upscale restaurant then in a nightclub or sports bar. See also **Back**.

- **Chiller** - The air conditioner.

- **Club Soda** - A flavorless, carbonated mixer, also referred to as soda water.

  > Some cities, particularly on the East Coast, refer to cola (Coke) as "soda." When mixing drinks, soda refers to SODA WATER or CLUB SODA. When in doubt, ask your customer which they mean.

- **Cocktail** - A mixed drink. Also a term for a cocktail waitress or waiter.

- **Cognac** - A brandy distilled in Cognac, France. Some of the most popular include *Courvoisier*, *Remy Martin*, and *Hennessy*.

- **Cointreau** - An orange flavored liqueur.

- **Colorado Bulldog** - The same drink as a Smith and Wesson. Colorado Bulldog is a popular name for the drink in the Midwest, while Smith and Wesson tends to be more common on the West Coast.

- **Cooler** - The large refrigerated storage area for restaurant food supplies and beer kegs.

- **Crème de** - Liqueurs made with fruits, berries and sometimes nuts. These sweet liqueurs are often used in exotic drinks or shooters. Some of the most common:

  - **Crème de Almond (Noyaux)** - A liqueur with a fruit punch flavor, used in a wide variety of exotic drinks, including Hurricanes, Mai-Tais, and Zombies.

  - **Crème de Banana** - A liqueur with a light banana and pineapple flavor.

  - **Crème de Cacao** - A chocolate flavored liqueur. This liqueur comes in two different colors, white (clear), or brown, and is common in coffee drinks and shooters.

  - **Crème de Coconut** - A liqueur with a strong coconut flavor, used in exotic drinks such as Piña Coladas and Bahama Mamas. This liqueur is very popular in drinks served in resorts, and Asian and Mexican restaurants.

  - **Crème de Menthe** - A peppermint flavored liqueur. Crème de Menthe comes in two colors, white (clear) and green.

  - **Crème de Café** - A coffee flavored liqueur.

  - **Crème de Cassis** - A liqueur has a strong black current flavor.

- **Crown** - *Crown Royal* Canadian whiskey.

- *Curacao* - An orange flavored liqueur, made on the Island of Curacao. Usually blue, it may come in a variety of other colors.

  Blue *Curacao* is used in making exotic drinks such as Blue Hawaiians and Blue Margaritas.

- **Cut Off** - A patron who is not allowed to have any more liquor for that day. Food, coffee, and cola may be recommended as alternatives.

- **Dirty** - A drink served with 1/4-1/2 ounce of green olive juice poured into it. This term is most often used in connection with martinis.

- **Draft** - Tap beer, served in a chilled glass.

- ***Drambuie*** - A brand of Scottish liqueur with the flavors of heather and honey.

- **Double** - Double the amount of liquor, but serve it in the same size glass. This gives a very strong drink, with just a little mixer. For example, a *"double rum and Coke"* means 2 ounces of rum and a little Coke in a bucket glass.

- **86'ed** - A patron who has become so unruly that they are barred from coming back into the bar. The barring may be temporary or permanent.

- **Electric** - A drink that is topped with 1/2 ounce of tequila. For example, an *"Electric Ice Tea."*

- **English** - A drink that is topped with 1/2 ounce of gin. For example, a *"vodka and tonic with a little English."*

- **First Call** - The notification to let guests know that the bar is now open to serve alcohol (usually 6 am).

- **Flair** - Serving drinks with an exceptional skill and show-manship delivery. May including fancy ways of popping tops off beer bottles, flipping and catching (the operative word here is – CATCH) bottles and glasses, even flipping and tossing fruit and ice.

\*\* Practice flair techniques at home before you try them at work. Don't try to show off too much. Better to simply serve customers well, then miss a catch and break several expensive bottles of liquor.

- **Flaming** - Drinks with a high alcohol content, which are lit, and then served while on fire.

> *In most states,*
> *flaming drinks are illegal to serve.*

- **Float** - The top 1/2-ounce of liquor or syrup "floated" on top of a drink, for example, a *"rum and Coke with a float of grenadine."* A float may also be referred to as a top, or a lid.

    Depending on the liquor, other terms may apply, such as screaming (vodka), electric (tequila), English (gin), multiple (*Frangelico*), and against the wall (*Galliano*).

- *Frangelico* - A hazelnut flavored Italian liqueur, packaged in a distinctive bottle shaped like a monk, complete with a rope belt.

- **Free Pouring** - A method professional bartenders use to measure liquor by counting or "feeling" when an ounce has been poured. Good bartenders can free pour accurately with both hands simultaneously. Special pour spouts to control liquor flow from the bottle are normally used.

- *Galliano* - A brand of licorice and vanilla flavored liqueur, sold in a distinctive, long neck bottle. The neck is so long that bartenders tend to knock over the bottle when they reach for nearby liquors. As a precaution, *Galliano* is stored against the wall. This explains the term "Against the Wall," which means to add *Galliano* to a drink.

- **Gin** - Liquor similar to whiskey, which has been flavored with Juniper berries.

- **Gold (Golden)** - The term "gold" usually refers to tequila that has been aged in oak whiskey barrels. For example, *Jose Cuervo Gold.*

  "Gold" may also refer to a drink made with gold tequila, such as a Gold Margarita.

- *Goldschlager* - A Swiss cinnamon liqueur that contains distinctive 24 karat gold flakes. *Goldschlager* is normally served chilled, and should be shaken to float the gold flakes.

  This liqueur is often used in shooters and coffee drinks.

- *Grand Marnier* - A French liqueur with strong orange flavors. *Grand Marnier* is often served heated.

- **Grenadine** - A non-alcoholic cherry flavored syrup made from pomegranates.

- **Head** - The foamy top of a beer.

- **Head** - A slang or street term for the restroom.

- **Heat** - Local police, liquor control board officers, or any undercover federal or county police officer. "The Heat's in the house," usually means Liquor Control is in the bar. As always, be sure to check ID on everyone.

- **Heater** - A bucket, or similar glass, filled with very hot water, and served with a snifter of brandy or cognac. The customer lays the snifter on top of the bucket glass to warm the brandy. Serve a fresh heater with each new brandy ordered.

> **Advise your cocktail person that the glass is HOT, as they may pick it up when serving and get burned, or not expect a hot glass and drop it.**

- **Hefeweizen** *(Hef)* - A popular German style beer. Hefeweizen is a thick, unfiltered beer that is slightly fruity tasting, and is served with lemon wedges.

- **Holy Water** - *Christian Brothers* Brandy.

- **Hurt Me** - A customer's request to pour the liquor a little extra heavy. For example, a *"gin and tonic, and hurt me."*

  "Hurt me" is a different term then "bite me," which is the verbal equivalent of flipping you off.

- **Irish Cream** - A chocolate and cream flavored liqueur made with an Irish whiskey base. Irish cream is especially popular in coffee drinks and shooters.

- ***Jagermeister*** - A popular German liqueur with the flavors of licorice and rootbeer.

- **Jigger** - An hourglass shaped measuring device, usually steel. The most common type measures 1 ounce on one side and 1-1/2 ounces on the other. Other measurements are available.

- ***Kahlua*** - A coffee flavored liqueur made in Mexico. *Kahlua* is very popular in coffee drinks and shooters. *Kapali* is the brand name of a similar, lower cost product.

- **Keg** - A metal container for holding tap beer. Full size kegs may weigh as much as 300 pounds. Smaller kegs are called Pony Kegs.

  Kegs must be kept cold. If the beer is allowed to get warm the flavor may change, and it will result in foamy pouring.

- **Kosher** - Products made following Jewish laws, and blessed by a Rabbi.

- **Last Call** - The notification, usually yelled across the bar or announced over the loud speaker, to let guests know it is getting close to closing time, or the time when the bar must stop serving alcohol. Customers are allowed to order <u>one</u> last drink. Some bars announce Last Call about half and hour before they have to pull the drinks, others may give Last Call as close as 10 – 15 minutes before closing.

- **Loaded** - A customer that has had too much to drink. Women may be referred to as "tipsy" (generally this would be said of an older woman), while men are generally referred to as loaded, smashed, lit or overdone.

- **Lid** - The 1/2-oz of liquor or syrup floated on top of a drink. The lid is often a contrasting color to the main drink, and is added for both taste and appearance. For example, a Mai Tai is made with a dark brown lid of *Myers'* rum.

    A lid may also be referred to as a top or a float. Depending on the liquor other terms may apply, such as screaming (vodka), electric (tequila), English (gin), multiple (*Frangelico*), and against the wall (*Galliano*).

- **Light** - A match or cigarette lighter.

- **Light** - Serving a cocktail with slightly less alcohol than the drink normally requires. For example, a *"rum and Coke - light."*

- **Liqueur** - Liqueurs and cordials are made using a straight liquor base such as whiskey, gin or vodka, and distilling them with fruits, berries, nuts, flowers, twigs, etc. The result is a very flavorful, high sugar content liquor.

- **Mexican** - A drink topped with 1/2 ounce of tequila. For example, a *"Fuzzy Naval Mexican Style."*

- **Microbrewery** - Small, local breweries.

- *Midori* - A Japanese liqueur with the flavor of honeydew melon.

- **Multiple** - A drink topped with 1/2 ounce of **Frangelico**. For example, a *"multiple Smith and Wesson."*

- **Neat** - A drink served at room temperature with no ice.

- **151** - A high proof type of rum. 151 is highly flammable, and is often used in flaming drinks.

> ### In most states, flaming drinks are illegal to serve.

- *Ouzo* - A Greek liqueur with a strong licorice flavor. *Ouzo* is normally served chilled.

- **Permit to Serve Alcohol** (Over the Age of 21). This is a license granted by the State Liquor Control Board to allow bartenders, waiters and waitresses to mix, pour, and serve alcohol. It requires that you be **21 years of age or older**, (or the legal drinking age in your state.) You must take a class provided by a state-licensed instructor, and be tested on your knowledge of the state laws and regulations. The permit is valid for 5 years, and must be renewed prior to that time by retaking the class and re-testing. The permit can be revoked for violations of state laws, including DUI or drug related convictions, and serving violations - especially serving to minors.

- **Permit to Serve Alcohol** (Under 21 years of age). This is a license granted by the State Liquor Control Board to allow waiters and waitresses to *serve alcohol,* (**you are NOT allowed to mix or pour drinks, or act as a bartender).** It requires that you to be 18-21 years of age, (check with your particular State's laws). You must take a class provided by a state-licensed instructor, and be tested on your knowledge of the state laws and regulations. The permit is valid until you reach the age of 21. When you reach 21, you can automatically upgrade to the license designated for those over 21. Your permit can be revoked for violations of state laws, including DUI or drug related convictions, and serving violations - especially serving to minors.

- **Port Wine** - A sweet, dessert-type wine that has been fortified with brandy.

- **Pounder** - The large, heavy glass used to serve draft beer. This glass is called a "pounder," because it holds 16 ounces, or a "pound" of beer.

- **Press** - Short for "Presbyterian," a mixed drink made of liquor and a mixture of 1/2 Ginger Ale and 1/2 soda water.

- **Quinine Water** - Carbonated water containing a small amount of Quinine. Quinine water is also known as tonic water, and has a characteristic slightly bitter taste.

  Tonic water was originally used in the East Indies to fight Malaria.

  Tonic water is usually labeled on a speed gun as "Q," for Quinine.

- **Rocks** - Ice.

- **Rocks Glass** - A small glass used to serve 1 to 1-1/2 shot drinks, over ice (rocks). This glass holds about 5 ounces total.

- **Rose's Lime Juice** - A non-alcoholic lime flavored syrup, used in a variety of drinks, such as margaritas and Kamikazes.

- *Rumplemintz* - A high quality peppermint schnapps made in Germany.

- *Sambuca* - A licorice flavored Italian liqueur. *Sambuca* is normally served chilled.

- **Schnapps** - German style liqueurs that come in a wide variety of flavors, including peppermint, peach, apricot and blackberry.

- **Schooner** - A large, tulip shaped glass used in serving draft beer. A schooner holds about 16 ounces. Smaller versions are called Half Schooners.

- **Screaming** - A drink topped with 1/2 ounce of vodka. For example, a *"screaming Melon Ball."*

- **Shift** - A scheduled time for working.

- **Short** - A drink served in a smaller glass than is normally used. This gives a stronger drink, because of the reduced amount of mixer.

- **Short Shot** - Serving a cocktail or shot with slightly less alcohol then the drink normally requires. Short shots are usually charged at full price.

- **Shot** - A measurement equivalent to one ounce.

- **Shot Glass** - The small glass used to serve a straight shot of liquor.

- **Skimming** - A slang term for stealing from the cash register.

- **Sloe Gin** - A liqueur made from Sloeberries, a berry similar to a raspberry. There is no gin in Sloe Gin.

- **Snifter** - The bowl shaped glass used to serve brandy and cognac.

- *SoCo - Southern Comfort* liqueur.

- **Soda** - A flavorless, carbonated mixer, also referred to as club soda.

> Some cities, particularly on the East Coast, refer to cola (Coke) as "soda." When mixing drinks, soda refers to **SODA WATER** or **CLUB SODA**. When in doubt, ask your customer which they mean.

- *Southern Comfort* **(SoCo)** - A popular brand of liqueur with the flavors of apricot and peaches.

- **Splash** - A squirt of requested item, about 1/2 ounce, added on top of the drink. For example, a *"gin and tonic with a splash of 7-up."*

- **Splash** - A non-alcoholic blend of fruit juices and 7-Up, served over ice in a large glass.

- **Spritzer** - A light, refreshing drink made from a combination of 1/2 wine (any type, especially flavored wines) or champagne, and 1/2 club soda. A Spritzer is served in a tall glass, over ice.

    Some popular combinations include a White Wine Spritzer (made with White Zinfandel), a Red Wine Spritzer (made with Merlot or Cabernet Sauvignon).

    For a sweeter drink, try a Red Wine Spritzer made with port wine, or a 1/2 shot of brandy or other flavored liqueur.

- **Squeeze** - A technique for adding fruit juice to a drink.

- **Stoli** - *Stolichnaya* Vodka, a popular Russian vodka that comes in a variety of flavors. Some of the most popular are vanilla and raspberry.

- **Straight Up** - A drink that has been shaken or stirred with ice to chill it then served in a chilled glass, with no ice.

- **Tab** - A bar bill a customer may run for drinks and food. Most bars require the customer to secure the bill with a credit card.

- **Tall** - A drink served in a glass larger then the drink is normally served in. This means the drink has a less intense alcohol flavor because of the additional mixer.

- **Tequila** - A liquor made in Mexico from the distilled sap of the Blue Agave plant, which is similar to a cactus. In America, we know this plant as the American Aloe. To be called tequila, the liquor must be distilled near the city of Tequila, Mexico. Tequilas made elsewhere in Mexico are called Mescal.

  Tequila can be sold aged or unaged. Aged tequilas such as *Jose Cuervo Gold*, and *Cuervo 1800* are matured in used whiskey barrels, resulting in a mellower flavor and a soft golden color.

- **Tia Maria** - A coffee flavored Jamaican liqueur, similar to *Kahlua*.

- **Till** - The cash register.

- **Tip** - A payment made by a customer to a bartender or server in appreciation of service.

Remember: customers are not required to tip you. You need to EARN the tip with good service and a positive attitude.

- **Tonic Water** - Carbonated water containing a small amount of Quinine. Tonic water is also known as Quinine water, and has a characteristic slightly bitter taste.

  Tonic water was originally used in the East Indies to fight Malaria.

  Tonic water is usually labeled on a speed gun as "Q," for Quinine.

- **Top** - The 1/2-ounce of liquor or syrup floating on top of a drink. For example, a *"rum and Coke topped with grenadine."*

  A top may also be referred to as a lid, or a float. Depending on the liquor, other terms may apply, such as screaming (vodka), electric (tequila), English (gin), multiple (***Frangelico***), and against the wall (***Galliano***).

- **Topless** - A drink served without a salted or sugared rim. For example, a *"topless Bloody Mary."*

- **Training Wheels** - The lemon slices served with tequila.

- **Triple Sec** - An orange flavored liqueur, used in a wide variety of drinks from Exotics to margaritas and Long Island ice teas. Triple Sec is usually found in the "well" or speed rack.

- ***Tuaca*** - An Italian liqueur with the flavors of caramel, vanilla, and fruit.

- **Turkey** - *Wild Turkey* bourbon

- **Unleaded** - A term that usually refers to decaffeinated coffee. When talking about a drink, it means a drink made with no alcohol.

- **Up** - Short for ***Straight Up***, a drink that has been shaken or stirred with ice to chill it, then served in a chilled glass, with no ice.

- **Velvet** - ***Black Velvet*** Canadian whiskey.

- **Virgin** - A drink made with no alcohol.

- **Well (Speed Rack)** - House liquors kept in a rack next to, or in front of, the bartender's ice. The most often used, and cheaper, house liquors.

- **Well Drinks** - Cheap drinks made from house liquors.

- ***Yukon Jack*** - A popular Canadian liqueur, often miscategorized as a whiskey. Yukon is considered a liqueur due to a very high sugar content.

- **Zin** – Short for Zinfandel wine.

# A Few Last Thoughts

While you may not ever work in a haunted bar, you will definitely have many exciting and fun adventures while bartending. Maybe you will work for a cruise line, and see the world. Or work in Las Vegas, Lake Tahoe, or New York City. Wherever you go, I hope that you find good people to work with, a full tip jar every night, and have lots of laughter (and really bad jokes) to share with your friends and family.

I am always interested in outrageous stories, new recipes, humorous jokes, and bad pick up lines.
Please feel free to email me at
**CdeLove@BartendingSupply.com**

For additional information on bartending and flair supplies, classes, and upcoming books, please visit:
**www.BartendingSupply.com**

Thank you.

# Sources Consulted

Adams, Cecil, "Will the quinine in tonic water prevent malaria?," *The Straight Dope, a division of Chicago Reader, Inc.*, 13 August 1999, <http://www.straight dope.com/classics/a990813.html>, (21 April 2004).

"Beefeater Gin," *Thomas Lowndes & Co. Ltd.* (a subsidiary of Allied Domecq Spirits & Wine Ltd.), <http://www.thomas lowndes.com/ beefeater.html>, (4 April 2004).

"Brief history of what a tequila drink is.," *PageWise, Inc.*, 2002, <http://wvvv.essortment.com/whattequiladri_ rdvx.htm>, (5 April 2004)

Chadwick, Ian, "From ancient pulque to today. Tequila's history and culture.," *The Cultured Traveler*, Volume 6, February 2004, <http://www.theculturedtraveler.com/Archives/ Feb2004/Tequila.htm>, (4 April 2004)

Clarke, Dan, "Tasting History, A Trip into Inglenook's Past," *California Wine and Food Magazine*, <http://www.californiawine andfood.com/wine/ inglenook-tasting.htm>, (28 April 2004).

"Clydesdale Stables, Grant's Farm," *Anheuser-Busch Inc.*, <http://www.grantsfarm.com/docs/stables.htm>, (1 May 2004).

"Common Wine Questions," *Gallo of Sonoma*, <http://www. galloofsonoma.com/wine_questions.asp>, (28 April 2004).

"Coors Brewing Company: Celebrating 125 Years of Brewing Excellence," *Rocky Mountain Beer Notes*, April 1998, <http://www.beernotes.com/rockymtn/ articles/ 000324.html>, (04 April 2004).

"Coors Organization/History," *Birmingham Beverage Company*, <http://www.alabev.com/coorsorg.htm>, (04 April 2004).

Deegan, Grant, "From the Bathtub to the Boardroom: Gin and its History," *Pimp Works*, <http://www.pimp works.org/~vincent/historymain.html#gin>, (15 April 2004).

"Drink Like 007," *M16 – The Home of 007*, 26th November 2002, <http://www.mi6.co.uk/sections/ articles/drink_like_007.php3?t=&s=articles>, (5 May 2004).

"Famous Budweiser Clydesdales," *Budweiser Company, a division of Anheuser-Busch Inc.*, <http://www.budweiser tours.com/docs/clydes.htm>, (2 May 2004).

"Gin and Tonic," *Science Daily LLC*, <http://www. science daily.com/encyclopedia/ gin_and_tonic>, (2 April 2004).

GNS, "Rum Lords: History of Bacardi Terror," *Hindustan Times Ltd*, 13 April, <http://www.hindustantimes.com/news/ 5922_680719,0015002100000 121.htm>, (30 April 2004)

Goldberg, Jonah, "Buds for life, A man and his beer," *National Review - Online*, 25 September 2000, <http://www.national review.com/25sept00/goldberg092500.shtml>, (3 May 2004).

"Guide to Food and Wine Pairing," *Chateau Ste. Michelle Winery*, <http://www.ste-michelle.com/ Sub_TraditionalPairings.cfm?>, (2 May 2004).

Hanik, Mariab, "History of Vodka, Origin, Name and Distilling in Poland," <http://www.polishvodka.com.pl/ history-vodka/title-page.htm>, (3 April 2004).

"Hydroplane racing - Miss Budweiser shatters world speed record for kilometer run," *Detroit News Motor Sports*, 14 March 2004, <http://www.detnews.com/ 2004/motorsports/ 0403/17/motorsports-91404.htm>, (14 April 2004).

"James Burrough – the Founder," *Beefeater Gin*, <http://beefeatergin.com>, (15 March 2004).

"King of Beers – History Timeline," *Budweiser Company, a division of Anheuser-Busch Inc.*, <http://www.budweiser. ca/kob_history.html>, (25 April 2004).

"Make Mine a 007 – The James Bond Films," *The Minister of Martinis*, 2002, <http://home.earthlink.net/ ~atomic_rom/007/films.htm>, (5 May 2004).

Melhoff, Craig, "Cure for what ails you? Why gin and tonic isn't covered by your medical benefits," *The National Pist*, <http://www.pist.ca/news/gin.html>, (3 April 2004).

"Our Wines," *Gossamer Bay Vineyards*, <http://www. gossamerbay.com/wines.html>, (21 April 2004)

Prokaziuk, Michael, "Vodka: From Peter the Great to Peter the Polluted," *Pimp Works*, <http://www.pimp works.org/~vincent/ historymain.html#vodka>, (15 April 2004).

Richardson, Paul and Ivanov, Mikhail, "The Little Water of Life," *Vodkaphiles (sponsored by Russian Life magazine)*, http://www.vodkaphiles.com/vodhis1.cfm, (3 May 2004).

Smith, Brian, "The History of Bacardi Rum," *PageWise, Inc*, 2002, <http://md.essortment.com/ historybacardi_ rwng.htm>, (6 March 2004).

Smith, Brian, "The history of vodka," *PageWise, Inc.*, 2001, <http://txtx.essortment.com/vodkadrinks_rbov.htm>, (14 April 2004).

Sorgatz, Dr. Andreas, "My Whiskey Notes...," *Sci-Face, Inc.* <http://math-www.uni-paderborn.de/~andi/ WHISKY/NOTE /index.shtml>, (5 May 2004).

Sorgatz, Dr. Andreas, "A Glossary of Whiskey Terms...," *Sci-Face, Inc.* <http://math-www.uni-paderborn.de/~andi/ WHISKY/glossary. shtml>, (5 May 2004).

"Steve's Gay 90's Restaurant," *Puget Sound Pipeline Online,* <www.pstos.org/instruments/wa/tacoma/ gay90s.htm>, (21 April 2004)

"Tequila Mexico," *Mission Liquor and Tobacco,* 2003, <http://www.missionliquors.com/tequila/mexico-tequila.html>, (28 March 2004)

"The APBA Gold Cup. History - Powerboat Racing," *Hickok Sports*, <http://www.hickoksports.com/ history/pbgoldcup.shtml>, (25 April 2004).

"The History of Vodka," *Synertech International Corp.*, (a note on the website lists the original source as Nicholas Faith & Ian Wisniewski, Classic Vodka, 1997), <http://www.ivodka.com/ history.html>, (5 April 2004).

Thompson, Joe, "Steve's Gay '90s (Tacoma)," *Cable Car Lines in the Pacific Northwest*, <www.cable-car-guy.com/html/ccsea.html#steves>, (28 April 2004).

"Today in History March 28, A Baseball Brew*, " Library of Congress American Memory Collections,* <http://memory.loc. gov/ammem/today/mar28.html>, (21 April 2004).

"Today, the BACARDI Bat is a welcomed character in over 170 countries worldwide," *Bacardi Worldwide*, <http://www.bacardi. ca/batorigins.asp?cityID=1&ticket=>, (5 April 2004)

 "Tonic Water," *Science Daily LLC*, <http://www.science daily.com/encyclopedia/tonic_water>, (2 April 2004).

Tyson, Joseph A., "Tequila - The Essence of Mexico," *Los Cabos Magazine - Los Cabos Visitor's Guide,* <http://www. loscabosguide.com/tequila/tequila-history.htm>, (3 April 2004)

Washington State Liquor Control Board, *Handbook for Liquor Licensees*, 2004.

"Whiskey Terms & Definitions," *kc.rr.com/mashbill*, <http://home.kc.rr.com/mashbill/ whiskey_terms.htm>, (28 April 2004).

"Why did James Bond want his martinis shaken, not stirred?," *The Straight Dope*, 28-Nov-2000, <http://www.straightdope. com/mailbag/mmartini.html>, (5 May 2004).

"Wine Basics," *Almaden Vineyards*,<http://www. almaden.com/ winebasics/whatsinthewine.htm>, (24 April 2004).

# Additional Sources

This section is made up of a wide variety of fun and interesting web resources. For most of these sites, you must be 21 or over to enter.

## Beer:

1. www.brewpubzone.com          (Beer Information)
2. www.budweiser.com          (Budweiser Information)
3. www.corona.com          (Corona Mexican Beer)
4. www.corona-extra.net          (Corona Mexican Beer)
5. www.coors.com          (Coors Brewery)
6. www.fosters.com          (Fosters' Brewery)
7. www.millerbrewing.com          (Miller Brewing Co.)
8. www.pyramidbrew.com          (Pyramid Ales Brewery)
9. www.redhook.com          (Red Hook Brewery)
10. www.washingtonbrewfest.com          (Beer Festivals)

## Brandy/Cognacs:

1. www.gallo.com          (E&J Brandy)
2. www.heaven-hill.com          (Christian Brothers Brandy)
3. www.hennessy-night.com          (Hennessy Cognac)
4. www.remy.com          (Remy Martin Cognac)

## Gin:

1. www.alcoholreviews.com          (Liquor Reviews)
2. www.beefeater.com          (Beefeater Gin)
3. www.beefeaterlondonradio.co.uk          (Beefeater Gin)
4. www.bestinwine.com          (Liquor Reviews)
5. www.bombaysapphire.com          (Bombay Gins)
6. www.drinksmixer.com          (Gin recipes)
7. www.ginvodka.org          (Gin and Vodka Information)
8. www.hawksburn.co.uk          (Hawksburn Gin)

9.  www.lankaproducts.com (Lanka Gin)
10. www.perryland.com (Gin Drinkers Club for Bombay Gin Enthusiasts)
11. www.71palm.com/MARTINIS.html (Martinis)
12. www.sikkimdistilleries.com (Sikkim Distilleries)
13. www.wineglobe.com (Liquor Information)

## Rum:

1.  www.bacardi.com (Bacardi Distilleries)
2.  www.cabanaboyrum.com (Cabana Boy Rums)
3.  www.gocaribbean.com (Caribbean Cruises)
4.  www.missionliquors.com (Liquor Information)
5.  www.mountgay.com (Mount Gay Rums)
6.  www.rum.com (Captain Morgan Rum)
7.  www.rum.cz (Rum Information)
8.  www.thedrinkshop.com (Rum Recipes)

## Tequila:

1.  www.cuervo.com (Cuervo Distilleries)
2.  www.ianchadwick.com (Tequila Information)
3.  www.lasmargaritas.com (Margarita Information)
4.  www.loscabosguide.com (Los Cabos Travel Info)
5.  www.mixed-drink.com (Tequila Recipes)
6.  www.theculturedtraveler.com (Travel Information)
7.  www.tequila-shots.com (Tequila Recipes)
8.  www.vivatequila.com (Tequila Information)

## Vodka:

1.  www.absolut.com (Absolut Vodka)
2.  www.honeyvodka.com (Honey Vodka Information)
3.  www.ivodka.com (Vodka Information)
4.  www.questia.com (On-Line library)
5.  www.smirnoff.com (Smirnoff Vodka)
6.  www.stoli.com (Stoli Vodka)
7.  www.skyy.com (Skyy Vodka)
8.  www.vodkaphiles.com (Vodka Information)

# Whiskey:

1. www.bushmills.com          (Bushmill's Irish Whiskey)
2. www.classicwhiskey.com          (Whiskey Information))
3. www.cooleywhiskey.com          (Cooley Whiskey)
4. www.jackdaniels.com          (Jack Daniel's Whiskey)
5. www.johnniewalker.com          (Johnnie Walker Scotch)
6. www.scotchwhisky.com          (Whiskey Information)
7. www.seagrams.com          (Seagram's Distillery)
8. www.seagram7.com          (Seagram's American Distillery)
9. www.vowhisky.com          (Seagram's Canadian Distillery)
10. www.whisky-tours.com          (Whiskey Distilleries)

# Wine:

1. www.americanwineries.org          (Nat Assn of Wineries)
2. www.brcohn.com          (BR Cohn Winery)
3. www.columbiawinery.com          (Columbia Crest Winery)
4. www.coveyrun.com          (Covey Run Vintners)
5. www.gallo.com          (Ernest & Julio Gallo Winery)
6. www.gunbun.com          (Gundlach-Bundschu Winery)
7. www.inglenook.com          (Inglenook Wines)
8. www.napavintners.com          (Napa Valley Vintners)
9. www.silverlakewinery.com          (Silverlake Winery)
10. www.ste-michelle.com          (Chateau Ste. Michelle Winery)
11. www.valleywinetours.com          (California winery tours)
12. www.weekendwinery.com          (WA Wineries - good info)
13. www.winebrats.com          (Wine Information)
14. www.winepressnw.com          (Washington Wineries)
15. www.yakimacellars.com          (Yakima Cellars Vintners)
16. www.zinfandel.org          (Zinfandel lovers site)

# Other Fun Sites

1. www.baileys.com          (Bailey's Irish Cream Distillery)
2. www.bartender.com          (Bartender Magazine)
3. www.barnonedrinks.com          (Cocktail recipes)
4. www.beverage.allrecipes.com          (Cocktail recipes)

5. www.beveragerecipe.com        (Cocktail recipes)
6. www.cocktails.about.com        (Shooter recipes)
7. www.cocktailsinthemail.com      (Shooter recipes)
8. www.cocktailtimes.com          (Cocktail recipes)
9. www.cocktail.uk.com            (Cocktail recipes)
10. www.disaronno.com          (DiSaronno Amaretto)
11. www.greatrecipesonline.com      (Lots of recipes)
12. www.grand-marnier.com          (Grand Marnier)
13. www.jager.com        (Jagermeister Information)
14. www.jagermeister.com    (Jagermeister Information)
15. www.kahlua.com              (Kahlua Distillery)
16. www.milioni.com              (Galliano recipes)
17. www.123easyaspie.com           (Liquor recipes)
18. www.123beveragesguide.com      (Cocktail recipes)
19. www.seagramscoolers.com       (Seagram's Coolers)

## 3 "P"s

People
Parking
Pull-Tabs

## 4 "B"s

Be Happy
Be Grateful
Be Generous
Be Humble

LaVergne, TN USA
11 May 2010
182202LV00004B/4/A